A
SATISFIED
BLACK
WOMAN

Shayla Morris

DEC 2009

My Time Publications
2984 Spring Falls Dr
West Carrollton, OH 45449
www.mytimepublications.com

ISBN 10: 0-9820530-9-6
ISBN 13: 978-0-9820530-9-6
First Printing 2009
Library Congress Of Control Number: on file

Printed in United States of America

10 9 8 7 6 5 4 3 2 1

This is a work of fiction. Any references or similarities to actual events, real people, living or dead, or to the real locals are intended to give the novel a sense of reality. Any similarity in other names, characters, places and incidents are entirely coincidental.

DEC 2009

ACKNOWLEDGMENTS

I would like to acknowdge my best friend, Angela, who reminded me of a talent that I've always loved to do. Thanks for the push.

And to the late Joseph M., a wonderful, earthly father who passed on his habits and love of writing to his baby girl.

And, to the best editor and publisher, Leila Jefferson, who is making a dream come true.

CHAPTER ONE

Thinking Back, Reminiscing

There was something sensual about staring out the window while the rain was falling. Hearing the droplets of water tapping on the windowsill helped me collect my thoughts to unleash my innermost feelings. A mood was set for whatever I could be thinking at the time. I looked around at my name plate that sat on my desk, *Shante Brenin, Senior Accountant.*

I started thinking about how happy I was with the decisions I'd made in life. I had asked myself several questions on numerous occasions. *Did I make the right choices? Should I have gone straight to college right after high school? Should I have waited a little longer to have gotten married? Should I have had kids right after graduation?*

At twenty five, I still had not had a baby. Unfortunately, that part of my life had already been chosen for me because of an emergency hysterectomy that was performed at the very young age of nineteen. But, if things would have been different, I think I would have had at least one child for Melvin if I'd met him a little earlier. Who was I fooling? I would not have spread my legs for anyone at that time either, although, in between my legs it felt like a leaking time bomb with hot, virgin juices brewing away within me, slowly cascading down my velvet walls, waiting to be released upon an eruption. My strict upbringing gave me a conscience to hold on tightly to my untouched goodies. But, if things turned out different and I did have a baby before nineteen, being unwed and all, Ma would have had my head.

My parents, Johnny and Aretha Evans, were definitely from the old school with raising my sister, Sharise, and I. We called my mother Ma and my father was known to us as Da. My parents originally come from Orange, Virginia. They got married and moved to the nation's capital, Washington, D.C., in 1964, where Sharise and I were born. Even though we were born there, I knew people thought the two of us as being southern because we carried the accents of certain words, like the names we used when we called out our parents. We were so used to those names that we always used them. Ma and Da were down to earth about a lot of things, but even to their standards, certain things were wrong to do. If I wasn't such a goody two shoes at times, there might have been a slight chance that I would have had a baby. I would have made them proud grandparents and my glorious sister an aunt. Would they have loved the child any less just because their strict rules weren't followed? But, it was no use of me crying over spilled milk. There was no big, red, shiny do over button that I could push. My life was what it was.

I started thinking about how eager my generation was. We were all so ready to fly the coop and get those apron strings cut from our parents. Da worked very hard for us to keep a roof over our heads and food on the table. Clothes were bought at a minimal. If you needed them, then you would get them, not as a fashion statement, but as a necessity. Sharise was three years older than me and was always content with the bare minimal that Da provided us with. She was a little lazy and didn't scream out for her independence, but I was different. So, when I got into the twelfth grade, after Da's permission, I took an after school job at Macy's.

CHAPTER TWO

Growing Up Smelling Myself

Two months had passed and I had been working at Macy's in the juniors department as a sales consultant. I was really excited that I was placed in that section of the store because I had access to all the latest fashions when they first arrived. I had really been working hard and I had grown to love the little money I made. The job helped me achieve a savings for fun and for my future.

Sharise was enjoying it also. Imagine that, she loved my money. I was very generous, but the time had come that I had to cut her back. I had to stop her from borrowing money from me, especially since she could never repay me, but I loved my sister so I would give her money out of a necessity. I think that I was turning into Da and maybe Sharise was more like Ma, being comfortable with someone taking care of her. But, Ma deserved it. Besides, she was his wife, and I hoped Sharise would find someone who was like Da that would take care of her.

When my mind was set on that type of thinking I realized my identity had been born. I was ready to be independent. I saved hard for anything I wanted and pretty much achieved my goals. I remembered those leather penny loafers from Hahn's shoe store that I wanted so much. At the time, everybody was wearing them with straight legged Calvin Klein Jeans. They were the bomb and I finally saved enough money to get them. Working at Macy's kept me current in all the styles with my classmates, even the popular ones. I mean, it didn't make me one of them, but I was sure as hell going to look like one of them, with good grades and all. I guess I should have been satisfied with that, but like a drug addict trying a new drug, I got addicted and wanted more. I felt like I had to get to the next level.

I got more flirty attention from the fellows, which swelled my head a bit. I finally felt pretty, attractive, and knew that I had it going on. No longer did classmates tease me for having crooked legs which they never understood. They now saw shapely, sexy, curved legs with a bow right in the middle of them. I wasn't conceited, but when I wore my shorts and miniskirts, I would think to myself, *Damn, my sexy ass bows are getting all the attention again.*

The time had come that I wanted to be in the big leagues. The world and its influences were slowly pulling me to live of the world and not in the word as I had been taught. I wanted to know what it felt like to be a real woman. My hormones were racing and my body was changing. Ma would use the term 'smelling themselves' about girls coming of age. Up to this day, I really don't know what that meant, but I would think in today's terms it would mean that you were growing up hot and horny. I guess I was smelling myself for real.

I started to put my sex appeal out there, to add fuel to the fire so to speak. I had a perfect little ass, in today's term, a perfect apple bottom, which looked real good in anything I wore. The guys were not hesitant to let me know it either with the whistling and calling me as I passed by. "Shorty, Shooooooorta, you got a minute?" I'd blush, smile, and keep on switching as I walked by. I loved the attention, but they made me nervous as hell. My classmates were not the only ones that gave me attention; the older men were coming on board, too. It was a different feeling, and a little scary at times. Their demeanor was very serious and some would even get annoyed if I brushed them off. I learned they could be just as conniving as females to get what they wanted. Mr. Hayes, my algebra teacher, was the perfect example.

The reputation that followed him was that he was tough on his students and he gave out very difficult lessons to pass. In addition to that, he would always sit girls with dresses or skirts on the front row in class. His explanation was that he wanted to prevent anyone from cheating, so anyone he thought may cheat, he would move, but in was mighty funny how his suspicions fell only on females who just so happened to be wearing a miniskirt or dress. When he sat at his desk to start class, his peeping Tom moment would arrive. Sometimes, I thought your grade was based on how you sat there. If you wanted an A, you knew just how far apart to part your legs to give him a good view as you sat at your desk.

I never had to worry about that until I started wearing my new outfits to class. When my miniskirts came into algebra class with me, all of a sudden I was moved to the front of the class. I always received a B average, but my skirt must have really shocked Mr. Hayes. On that particular day he felt it necessary that I be moved to the front. I asked him why and his response was for me not to ask questions but to just do as I was told. The class chanted the, "Oooohhhh." I walked up to the front and replaced Tony in the front row. Mr. Hayes stood up and started passing out a surprise test. There was a serious of, "Dangs," and moans of displeasure about it, but being in there, a test could be given at any moment.

"There will be absolutely no talking while taking this test. You will have twenty minutes," Mr. Hayes instructed us while he looked at the clock on the wall. "Begin."

There were five problems to solve. The first three were pretty easy, but the next two I had to take a little more time to figure out. I was in deep thought as I glanced from my paper, looking at the $y=(x+6)(6x)$ x to the second power; Mr. Hayes was in a trance with my legs as though he was mentally trying to make them open for him. Once our eyes met, he secretly moved his forefinger from side to side, giving his approval for me to open my legs for him. I never listened to the rumors about him, but I guess all the stories I had heard about him weren't all lies. He was a nasty, old pig to me at that point. I gave him a good rolling of my eyes and kept my knees tightly together, never giving in. He seemed frustrated, looked at the clock and told us to put our pencils down, then came by our desk and collected papers. He looked at me as though he couldn't stand me at that point. It was definitely an uncomfortable moment until the bell rung, releasing us from class. I started gathering all of my stuff together and was headed for the door when Mr. Hayes called me, so I turned around and went back to his desk. I didn't know why everyone seemed to be disappearing and left the two of us in there. He went through the test papers pulling mine, asking me what seemed to be the problem with my answers.

"I know we have been over this material before in class, where was your head at today?" he asked seriously. I couldn't believe it.

"Look, Mr. Hayes, I know that I had all of those problems correct. It took me a while on the last two, but it came back to me about solving those problems. Tell me what I did wrong. And, how would you even know something is wrong if you haven't even looked at my paper yet? The question we should be asking here is where your head was at today besides peeking?" He gave me a look that made me think he was going to start swinging on me, so I stepped back. Mr. Hayes' second period class was coming into the room, and he looked at me and told me that the afternoon would be a better time to talk. "I cannot stay after school for something that you have not even given me a reason for. Tell me now what this is about or you will not see me in here after school. I have a job that I have to go to." My voice had escalated and he was getting hot tempered with me. I figure it was because I was showing him up in front of everyone. Our conversation was getting the attention of his next class that had started filing into their seats. He got up and with me following him into the hallway.

"If you don't show up this afternoon you'll be sorry." I looked at him and told him that I'd take my chances. I left and hurried to my next class, all the while with Mr. Hayes steadily on my mind. Now I knew why some men with personal agendas scared me, they came on too strong. They would sometimes put wishful thinking into action no matter what the outcome might be. Sometimes, it was a man's desires that drove them to do foolish things. Some of them would deal with the consequences later, just as long as they got what they wanted. It could be right or wrong.

The next day, Mr. Hayes was a little late coming into class, and I sat back in my normal seat in the third row. My mind started drifting off again and I started feeling poetic, so I took the opportunity to scribble sweet words together. It was my favorite thing to do. I was always the one who stayed on balance, but lately, with all the attention, my balance was getting a little off. I remembered on that day in particular, my balance was knocked off and was put back in line very quickly. I started writing intimate thoughts that I was having at the moment. I wrote,

A satisfied Black Woman
Will I ever know?

I didn't know where it came from, and I was not at liberty to answer the question at that point in my life. But, little did I know, the first two lines were laying a carpet into my life as well as an entryway into my soul. I started with hopes of finishing it right away, but it would never be finished until I could live through the question and answer it honestly with an experienced walk through of life. Disappointments would also accompany the journey of finding the answer, as I found out that day in Algebra class.

The final bell was ringing and my concentration was broken when Eric King, the star quarterback of the football team, sat at his desk in front of me. Eric was every girl's dream, even though he was going out with Wanda Smith, the captain on the Varsity cheerleading squad. All I could do was gaze at the back of his well groomed head and fantasize, and then I started writing down what I was thinking. I wrote of Eric touching me, not with the roughness he showed on the field, but with tenderness you would give someone you loved. I started doodling drawings along with my writing, which on that particular day got me into trouble. Mr. Hayes had come in and started lecturing on lesson ten from the book. I was so far gone into my thoughts that I had not even noticed him standing there. Everyone was writing notes but me because my mind was still in the clouds. My formula only equaled to Eric and me. Mr. Hayes stood over me, zapping me out of my zone. He snatched up my paper, glanced over it, then looked directly at the back of Eric's head. He looked me straight in my eyes and deep down in my gut, I knew what his next move was going to be, his payback for the day before. He started reading my secret feelings I had for Eric out loud to humiliate me in front of the class. There was a bunch of laughter with a bunch of 'oohs' and 'ahhs' from the class. I couldn't even look at Eric as Mr. Hayes sent me down to Mr. Tuckerman's office who called my Ma. Check mate, Ma had the last move of punishment.

After that day, I restrained from writing any of my thoughts that came to my mind. One day, I hoped to be an aspiring poet and I would let the world know how I felt. But, at that time, the humiliation that Mr. Hayes made me feel was too fresh and painful to deal with. I had to erase the embarrassment that he made me feel, continue on with my thoughts, and keep them to myself, especially while I was in school.

CHAPTER THREE

Curiosity

My curiosities were still raging and I started wondering how it felt to have a man physically kiss and touch me. I listened to songs and felt as though they were singing to me personally, like Marvin Gaye telling me that he wanted me, or Barry White telling me that he couldn't get enough of my love. I wanted what everybody else was getting and I wondered how it felt to make love and feel a man inside me. I thought about it all the time. I figured that was normal being eighteen and still a virgin. My curiosities were short lived when coming home one night from work I accidently walked in on Sharise and her boyfriend, Vance, on the couch. I walked in quietly because all the lights were out and I didn't want to wake anyone. I closed and locked the front door. As I approached to reach for the lamp that stood on a hall stand outside the family room, I heard moans from Sharise, and Vance telling her that he loved her pussy.

She moaned again and then he asked her, "Whose pussy is this, Sharise?"

She answered him with, "Yours, baby, yours."

I knew I should have moved on, but I had to see, so I hit the light switch. They both were shocked and completely taken by surprise. He withdrew from her with his manhood still fully erect and glistening wet from my sister's tunnel. My eyes were fixated on them, not from a lust of wanting, but I was just stunned from the whole situation. Sharise screamed my name.

"Shanteeeee. Get out, damn."

Vance looked at me and told me to get the fuck out. "Damn, girl, my shit was about to..." Sharise pushed him away and told him he had to go.

My eyes were wide open. I got a grip on myself and mumbled

"Sorry," then ran up to my room and closed my bedroom door. I was lost for words and I had to give my brain a few minutes to regroup on what I had just seen. I didn't know why, but I felt so guilty about what just had happened. I shouldn't have felt that way, but at that time I did. I should have regrouped and put the blame where it rightfully belonged. Besides, I was not the one caught on my hands and knees, doggy style on the couch with Vance behind me with his dick in me. Sharise was totally wrong for disrespecting my parents' home that way. Shortly after that, I heard Vance leaving out of the front door, swearing under his breath. I then heard Sharise coming up the stairs. When she reached the top of the stairs, she paused as though she would come into my room like she always did almost every night. But, that night was different, she went into her room without even coming to say goodnight. I knew she felt guilty because Ma and Da were at church. Sharise probably thought that I was attending with them, but she learned different from the moment I switched the lights on and saw the two of them. Still although scandalous in my mind, I couldn't stop thinking about it. After that night, Sharise and I never discussed what had happened. It was like whatever happened on that couch stayed there and we never brought it up again.

As time passed on, that night was slowly erasing from my mind. The only time it refreshed was when Vance came around the house, which was becoming more often. He and Sharise were getting serious with each other. It was something about him though, that rubbed me the wrong way. He started staring at me, especially when no one else was around. I could feel his eyes burning a hole through my clothes. Sometimes he would try to brush up against me when no one was looking. I honestly wished he wasn't around so much, but I loved my sister and didn't want to ruin any happiness for her, so I kept it all to myself.

CHAPTER FOUR

Nothing Last Forever

Prom was approaching fast, just around the corner. That took my mind off things at home and made me excited about the upcoming events for my graduation class. Troy Evans asked me to be his date for the prom, so I accepted because I felt pretty safe with him. We had known each other since elementary. Troy lived around the corner on Fifth and Girad Street and he knew my entire family as I knew his, so I really felt good that I was going with him. It would be my first date and I had spent a whole month just preparing for it. Our prom was going to be held on the Spirit of Washington, a dinner cruise ship that cruised from the Potomac River, into the banks of Virginia, and back to the Potomac. I set money aside and got my dress custom made. It was a short dress with a small split on the side with spaghetti straps, so I wore a crocheted shawl. My heels were three inches high and you could not tell me anything. I tried the outfit on about twenty times, modeling for Ma, Da, and Sharise. They gave me much needed confidence on how I looked because I still had the jitters and nerves going on inside.

That much anticipated night came and it was time to go. Troy came to pick me up in a white limo. Da answered the door, "Hey, buddy, did you come here to get my baby girl?"

"Yes, sir."

"Boy, loosen up, I ain't going to bite you. Just don't have her out too late, now that's when I'll have to come looking for you."

"Yes, sir, I understand."

Troy was very nervous, but Da was just playing with him. I finally came down and Troy got up and opened the door for me. He wouldn't even check me out in my dress because he didn't want Da to think that his mind was in the gutter about me. Troy said he didn't know why he was so nervous, he has known my family most of his life, but that night was different. In the back of his mind, he really did have what most guys had on their mind about prom night, but I was not the one as he found out later.

We were in the limo for about five minutes and Troy was beginning to relax a bit. He turned to me and told me that there were going to be two other couples going with us. "I couldn't foot the whole bill by myself, so I asked Vincent Brown and Terrence Hall and their dates, Vanessa and Tamika, to ride with us.

"Okay," I quietly told him.

"Do you know them?"

"Yeah, I know of them, they are quite popular."

"Yeah they're alright. Relax, it seems like you are getting tense, it will be alright." Troy put his hand on mine. "Trust me." We drove around and picked up everybody, and they stepped in the limo sharp as they wanted to be. We all talked and had a good time, except for Venessa, who was Terrence's date. She was a pretty girl, but was stuck up as hell. Vincent turned on the stereo and cranked it up with the Junk Yard Band. We all were enjoying the sounds of D.C. Venessa sat like a log in her seat, rolling her eyes and snapping her mouth. She gave Terrance a look like she could just kill him.

We finally made it to the prom where I had the best time ever. It truly was a night to remember. Troy and I tore the dance floor up, but what happened at the end was even more memorable. Troy had told me that he was going to shoot the breeze with his home boys, so I sat down to rest my feet. Those heels were giving me no mercy from all the dancing that I had done. I had been sitting for about forty five minutes when I looked around for Troy and he was nowhere in sight. I kept glancing at my watch and saw that it was two thirty in the morning; I knew it was time for me to start getting home. I saw Vincent and Tamika still on the dance floor. Not too long after that, I saw Terrance coming up toward me with a lost look in his face.

"Hey, Shante, what's up?"

"Well I need to be getting back home, it's really getting late."

"Where is Troy?"

"I don't know, but can you walk me to the limo, maybe they will be heading back there."

"Okay, let's go."

"My feet are killing me. I don't think that I can make it back to the car."

"Well, why don't you take the heels off, it's pretty clean around here," Terrance told me. I slipped of the shoes and we walked, laughed, and talked all the way to the car. That night we found out that we had a lot in common. Terrance reached out for the door handle. "My lady, your chariot awaits." When Terrance opened the door, I stood frozen as Venessa's legs were spread eagle while Troy was eating her out. "Damn, dog, that's foul and messed up." My eyes were in disbelief. I backed away and asked Terrance to get me a cab. "Right, I'll be riding with you." Terrence turned around to Troy. "Dude, how could you do this? You know that Venessa and I are talking. And, how could you disrespect Shante like this?"

Venessa was crying, trying to get out of the limo. Troy had did a three sixty. I never saw that side of him. He pulled his pants up and went behind Terrance. I screamed because all I saw was a swing and he knocked Terrance down from behind.

"No, stop, Troy, what are you doing?" Soon after that, out of nowhere, at least three more guys came up and started pounding Terrance while he was down. I yelled for help, but my screams seem to be unheard. Shortly after that, I saw Troy pull a gun and point it at Terrance. I broke through the guys and threw myself on Terrance. "Please, Troy, don't do this." I begged him mercifulness not to shoot the gun. Troy looked in my tear soaked eyes and put his gun away.

"Come on, let's leave this punk ass nigga alone." They all started walking away. I turned to Terrance and looked at the damage they had inflicted on him. The police and ambulance soon arrived.

Terrence looked at me. "Why did you do something so stupid?"

"I don't know. I couldn't bear anything to have happened to you, especially after you stood up for me at the car. I think that we are going to be friends for a long time." I called my Da and we stuck to a story of not knowing who did the beating.

I left that incident behind me and tried to focus on graduation, which was three weeks away, and I couldn't wait to make my parents proud.

Friday evening had come around and we were at home helping prepare dinner. Ma had prepared her famous macaroni and cheese, I was frying chicken in the large, cast iron frying skillet, Sharise was stirring some fried corn, and Ma was checking in the oven on her biscuits. She would never finish any dinner off without those biscuits, which were the best biscuits around. Vance was on the front screen porch looking at the old nineteen inch television out there while he swatted at flies. We were having a good time discussing old times when the phone rang. It was a phone call that we would never dream of getting. I'll never forget that day. It was the tenth of May, 1993. That day seemed to stand still in my mind when I thought on it. The phone rang, and my mom answered and listened to the person on the other end. She stared into space, dropped the phone, and fainted. Sharise screamed as we both ran over to her. Vance came in off the porch and took my mother to the couch. I picked up the receiver and it was the police informing us that Da had just been killed in a car accident. We all cried and moaned for what seemed like an eternity. My world had been crushed. My Da was gone.

Uncle Ricky and Aunt Martha came to help us in our time of need, but what does that term really mean? I wanted to have Da back again. My time of need was to make him proud of me now. My time of need was to laugh with him again. It was my first, personal main blow in life. I would never see my Da again.

I looked as though I had been sedated as I sat across from Da laid to rest in an all white, satin lined casket just two weeks before my graduation. I felt sick to my stomach, and wanted to die and go with him to a better place that the reverend preached about. My heart ached, and my nerves were gone from my body. As we stood up to take a last look before they finally closed the top and locked it, Ma grieved and cried for her love until she passed out. The nurses came and revived her with smelling salt. The choir sang *Precious Lord*, which instantly brought memories back to me about Da. I remembered him taking me to Rock Creek Park where he taught me to ride a bike and showed me how to fly a kite. And, most importantly, he taught me how to be responsible. I loved him so much and now he was gone. My tears started to roll more as the pall bearers came to take Da away to the Hearst. When they rolled him past us, Sharise fainted. When the nurses came to bring her around, we left and took Da to his final resting place.

A year had passed and we were all still at the original house that Ma was the sole owner of because of Da passing. Da left her with a good retirement plan and she would not have to worry about anything else in life, so we thought. But, we were on the outside looking in. It was unbearable for her to be without Da. She tried her best to manage to be strong for us, and we, in turn, were being very protective of her, trying to make her happy. I now know that we were trying to take his place, which didn't work. Not much longer, about six months later, Ma was gone, joining her Da in the afterlife. God rest her soul, she was not with us anymore, either. I think she died of a broken heart, and I knew that I would miss her, too.

She was a God fearing woman that always taught Sharise and I the right way to go. Most of the time I heard what she was saying and knew that she spoke nothing but the truth, but sometimes I chose to do things my own way. But, you best believe, I never let what she said go in one ear and out the other. At first I was stubborn and tried not to think about what she had told me, but as I had grown older and my life went on, her teachings and advice became first priority that I thought about before making a lot of major decisions. Sometimes I had a chance to go into my memories of those golden rules that I had been taught and applied them to some stupid decisions that I had made sometimes, and still would make in the future. I always learned from experience that if I were too hasty in making up my mind without any sensible thinking, Ma's number one rule of, 'A hard head would make a soft ass,' would come into play. God knows I'd made plenty of dumb decisions, enough to last me a life time, enough to be wearing plenty of padding from the numerous times I'd fallen on my ass. I laughed to myself sometimes, thinking of some of the things she would say. No matter how many rules Ma had under her roof, each one was treated as rule number one. They all stood equally the same with her; you stuck by the rules to accommodate it.

CHAPTER FIVE

Reminiscing On What Used To Be

I started drifting off in space again; back to girlfriends I went through high school with. Kim, Angie, and I had made a pact. Our plans were to go off to Baltimore and attend Morgan State University and our vision was to share an apartment together and gain our independence. Wow, that feeling of freedom was so close, we all could taste it. But, as time went on, that good taste was knocked out of our mouths. Life began to deal one card each from the deck of life. When Da died and never got to see me graduate, I lost my enthusiasm on any goals I had. School was the furthest from my mind.

Kim fell in love with Brian, a linebacker from our school football team. One thing led to the next with their hot little romance, and Kim got pregnant, getting pregnant five months shy of graduation and putting her part of the pact on the backburner of the stove. We were all there to lend our shoulders for her to cry on. With all that she had to think about with her baby, she was really confident that Brian would be there for her. It was funny how things changed so quickly, from her being a trophy piece for Brian to show off, to being labeled as the one who is giving Brian her ass when he wanted it, to being   ashamed of and put out of sight because of her pregnancy.

Brian earned a football scholarship at Frostburg and his family tried feverously to convince Kim that it would be better for everyone if she would let them take care of an abortion. They also were trying to save face because it was 1993, a time where it was still a little shameful if you got caught holding the goodies after a slip. Well, Kim was a strong willed girl and didn't let anyone convince her of what to do. She finally decided that she was going to try and raise the baby herself because she didn't want to interfere with Brian's school. She really had a good heart. Kim still felt a connection going on with her and Brian and he kept things smoothed over, giving her a sense of hope that he would come back and marry her, then maybe she could get her education as well. But, only time would tell and seal their fate. Brian finally left for Frostburg University and Kim was left trying hard to hold on to her dreams and take care of their son. Brian's family was helping her financially as long as she didn't make noise with threatening to take him for child support.

Angie went into real estate and was doing quite well herself. We were still cool to this day and hung out when we could. I didn't enter college as planned, but decided to take a rest from school and got hired as a receptionist at Dave and Donavan Associates, the company that I was presently with.

CHAPTER SIX

Blinded By Love

Sharise and I stayed in the house for awhile. Needless to say, after Ma was gone Vance eased his way in the house quite smoothly as well. Lord knows I knew Da and Ma were turning around in their graves about that situation. Vance had an easy ride of not paying any rent or helping out on the utilities or food. Sharise didn't ask me how I felt about it or anything. Staying over one night turned into two nights, then weeks, and the next to follow were months. He never stopped giving me that uneasy feeling when he was in my presence.

Sharise started drinking a little when Ma left us; she said it helped her to sleep at night. Things were just the opposite for me. I could not sleep and I had no type of comfort to fall on. I had to keep my door locked and my eyes open most of time when Sharise fell in a deep slumber. I started saving diligently enough money to get my own place. It was only a matter of time before I knew the situation was going to hit the fan and I was scared. I had never been apart from my sister, she was all I had left at the time, but I had to get out of that house fast.

Just as soon as I thought about something might happen between Vance and I, it did. I hated the way he looked at me, I hated the way he would slyly brush up against me in tight spaces, and to have my privacy was impossible with him living in the house. Any time I was in the bathroom or bedroom I had to lock the door, then place a chair up against it for added security. One particular night I was on my way in the front door from work. I saw all the lights out, so as always, I came into the house very quietly. I was having hunger pains, so instead of going straight upstairs I made my way to the kitchen where I turned the lights on and went looking in the fridge for a small snack. I bent over, pulling out a small cup of Jello snacks. Being so hungry, I started opening the seal before I got my head up out of the door. When I stood up and turned around, Vance was right there in front of me, I never heard him when he came up behind me. My Jello had hit the floor and splattered over the bottom of the fridge and the cabinetss. From Vance's body being so close to me, I bumped into him. He came up closer to me and made sure that I felt his semi hard on that he had. I pushed him away.

"Damn it, Vance. Why are you sneaking up on people?"

He had the same sinister look in his eyes that he always had, along with a devilish grin on his face. He backed up. "Sorry. You need to be more careful at how you do things in the kitchen. Did you find anything interesting down here?" He looked down toward his dick. I knew what he was trying to get at, but I ignored him and started cleaning up the mess. I wondered where Sharise was, but then I realized that she probably took medication before she went to bed. She would hear nothing for a while. Vance just stood there and watched me clean up the mess. As hungry as I was, my appetite was gone. The only thing that I was thinking at that moment was I had to hurry up and save more money so I could start apartment hunting. I went upstairs, locked my door, and started crying. I really could not believe that Sharise had allowed an outsider to come into our family home and allow such behavior. I had to talk to her about it, but as usual, I was trying not to make any waves between my sister and I.

The next day came and I awoke to Vance and Sharise downstairs arguing. I sat up in the bed, looked toward the door, and noticed some envelopes had been slid underneath my door into my room. I figured it was my mail. When I got up to retrieve them, there were four envelopes, each in its own bright color to let you know that it was a cut off notice. In yellow WSSC, the water company had sent a notice a week ago. In blue Pepco, the electric company sent a notice in a bright shade of blue with a turn off date in five days. Washington Gas Company was in a normal envelope and was on time because I usually paid that. And the telephone bill, which was rather thin, was a cut off notice as well. Sharise worked downtown with AT&T as a receptionist and she made a decent salary. We would always spit the utilities but since Vance moved in, I felt it only fair for him to foot some of those bills. To make things look better for him as a man, Sharise would always tell me that he was paying their half, but I knew it was a lie. She was paying everything; she just wanted me to think otherwise.

When I came downstairs the arguing stopped. Vance looked

over toward me coming down the stairs, grabbed his jacket, and said he was going to work. Sharise and I went in the kitchen, and she looked at me carrying the bills in my hand. I laid them on the table and asked Sharise what it was about, then poured myself a cup of coffee and waited for her explanation. She explained she had started getting a little behind on things because she started missing work a lot. We sat at the table from each other and Sharise didn't look good to me. It looked as though she hadn't had any sleep, and she seemed very tired. I told her that we needed to talk about the bills.

"Who put these under my door? I mean, look, we had an agreement. It's only fair that Vance help out with the bills. I mean, ever since he's been here it seems as though everything is falling apart with you, Sharise."

She looked at me and started crying. "Shante, I'm pregnant. Vance said now he has to save all his money for the baby. He said that we are going to get married, so I put his name on my savings and checking and made it a joint account. That's why we haven't paid our share of the utilities. We need to save everything."

I was shocked and couldn't believe what I was hearing. I hoped that Vance was not setting her up and planned to take all of her money, but I didn't want to continue arguing with her. I embraced my sister and told her that everything was going to be alright, but in the back of my mind, I still wanted to know what Vance's intentions were. I wanted to tell Sharise about all his backstabbing, but it would not be a good time. I didn't want to upset her, but I knew that my next talk would be with Vance. I couldn't stand it any longer. It was my parents' house and they left it for Sharise and I, not that nigger who was really getting on my nerves. It was time for us to talk. I wanted to know what happened to the money that I had given Sharise last month for my half of the utilities. I always gave her cash and she would normally deposit the money, write the check, and pay the bill. I knew that they didn't expect me to pay all the utilities and they didn't contribute to anything. I didn't know who put the bills under my door, but I was soon to find out after Vance got home from work that day. It was going to me and him. Sharise and I left for work together.

The hour had finally arrived that I had been waiting for all day. The sound of the front door closing behind me was the greatest; I was finally home from a long day. I went toward the kitchen and it was torn up.

Damn, pots and pans filled the sink. The stove contained pots that still had food in them and there were plates on the table with food. I went to see if Sharise was at home, I figured maybe she wasn't feeling well. I called her from the bottom of the steps, then I thought that maybe she was sleep so I should check in on her. I went up the stairs and her bedroom door was barely closed. I reached for the knob and heard stirring inside as though she may be taking a nap. I stopped myself because it could have been Vance inside as well; it was hard to break old habits of just barging in on my sister when it was just her room. I withdrew my hand quickly from the door knob and called out to her.

"Sharise, are you home?" I got no response so I left without opening the door and went back downstairs to take care of the mess in the kitchen. I started washing the dishes, and then suddenly I heard the front door close. "Sharise, Vance, is that you?" There was no answer. I was getting a little nervous, suppose someone had got into the house?

I picked up a knife off the counter that I had just washed and dried. When I looked out the door toward the corner, I saw Vance walking fast with a girl, trying their best to get out of view. I couldn't believe him, I knew he must had been upstairs with her. He was a motherfucking dog, fucking some low life, stupid bitch in our house. I was struck with grief and hurt for my sister. I knew the news would almost kill her, but I didn't know if I should tell her because I was thinking of the baby. As tears streamed down my face, I looked down on the floor and there was a steam of blood dripping from my hand. The intensity of knowing about Vance with that girl cheating on my sister struck a nerve in me so bad that I forgot I was even holding the knife and cut my fingers. I ran to the bathroom and attended to my wounds, knowing I would be stuck with that on my mind the rest of the evening.

When five thirty came, Sharise was walking in the door from work. She seemed to be in a good mood and started telling me about her day. I told her about mine, minus the part about me coming home early; we went into the kitchen and started dinner. Not too long after, around six, Vance was coming in from his job. He came into the kitchen and kissed Sharise and her stomach. He made me sick just looking at him. He looked up toward me as though he knew that I knew about his day and dared me to say anything. Besides being a dog, he was also a cocky motherfucker. I couldn't wait to get a chance to talk to him without Sharise, to tell his ass to get out or straighten up.

We ate roast beef, potatoes, and string beans for dinner. Sharise was full and satisfied and said she was really tired, so she went upstairs early and Vance was right behind her. I started washing the dishes and it wasn't long after when I heard someone coming back downstairs. It was no surprise that it was Vance. I was sure curiosity was killing him inside about just how much I knew or if I had seen anything earlier. I sat down at the table because all the dishes were done and he went to the sink and placed a dirty plate in it. I knew he didn't just do that.

"Excuse me, Vance, but do you see that I have just cleaned every dish in the sink? Can you please take a little time and wash that plate you just put in a clean sink, dry it off, and put away in the cabinet?"

"Oh, my bad," he said as he turned around, turned on the water, and washed it the plate. He reached for a towel, dried it, and placed it in the cabinet. "Are you happy now?" he asked in a sarcastic way. He came over and sat down at the table with me, making my skin crawl even more. He belonged in a pit of snakes. "You look like you got something serious going on in that head of yours. You okay?" he asked me.

I looked at him and started asking him about the bills that were shoved under my door that morning. "Vance, when I got up this morning I had all the utilities bills under my door. Do you know anything about that? Who put them there, and why weren't they paid? I gave my half of the money for the utilities. The money is gone, yet, none of them were paid and now we have a rack of cut off notices. What happened to the money that I left in the envelopes?" Vance looked at me and said that he really didn't know what I was talking about. I then told Vance that the money couldn't have vanished in thin air. "Where is the money for your half for the utilities?"

Vance looked at me and said that the money was put in the envelopes. "Since your sister was not feeling well, we didn't think that you would mind taking the bills to the bank today. But, we put our portion in and we put it under the door."

"Well, Vance, the bills were certainly there, but the money was not." Vance looked at me and told me that he just couldn't understand what could have happened to the money, and then looked at me and asked what was I insinuating. I shook my head and told him that the bills were still due. I wanted to move on and ask him about the day's events. "Okay, Vance, I'm ready to talk about today."

He looked at me. "What about today?"

I was pretty sure that Sharise was asleep by now; at least I prayed that she was. "Look, Vance, don't act stupid. I know you are aware that I was here when you had someone in here with you." He was looking at me as though he didn't know what I was talking about. I didn't want to beat around the bush, so I told him that I was home earlier when he had his little tramp in the house. He looked me straight in the eyes and told me that I didn't know what I was talking about. Vance was putting on as though he was an angel. I had to break through the coolness and let him show his true colors, along with the truth. I had to get down to his level. "Look, Vance, I know you were in this house fucking some slut face whore, disrespecting my sister in her own home, so don't try to deny it. I should go and have a talk with Sharise right now so she can throw your sorry ass out. You ain't nothing but a useless pair of pants. Maybe she will see you for what you really are. Number one, you are a no good motherfucker who steals from his own household, number two, you fuck sluts in your own woman's bed when she is not around, and number three, you will try to get ass from your girlfriend's own sister if allowed, but you can hang that one what up because that will never happen."

That was enough to start his fire. "Bitch, I don't need your god dammed money, I pay my bills. And you don't know what you're talking about, me fucking someone in here. I was not home today until late, my normal time at five thirty. Did you see me fucking somebody in here?" He was actually waiting for me to answer.

I guess our voices had risen so much that we woke up Sharise, who was standing in the doorway with dazed look on her face. I'm sure Vance wondered as much as I did how long had she been standing there and how much she had heard. I hated that I even brought the whole conversation up. I wanted him to know that I was aware of what was going on, but I wanted time to tell Sharise later, in a more subtle tone. It was not the right time for me to approach her. Vance and I both looked dumbfounded and I was feeling guilty of not telling her what was really going on.

"Baby, what are you doing up? Were we making too much noise that we woke you up?" Vance hugged Sharise and sat her down, then playfully started kissing on her.

Man, didn't he know that behavior was going to make her suspicious? I started a conversation with her, asking if she was hungry and wanted me to fix her something. Sharise held her stomach, shaking her head, telling me no. She told us that she wasn't feeling good.

"It seems as though I am spotting a little." Sharise had a tear in her eye. I never had experienced a pregnancy and neither had Sharise, but I did know with her mentioning spotting she would have to stay off of her feet, and then we needed to call her doctor. I didn't know if Sharise was worried about anything, so I prayed to God that I was not the cause of her spotting. I hoped she didn't hear the conversation between Vance and I. I made up my mind that I would never breathe a word to her about my suspicions of him if I could help it; I just wanted everything to be okay. I told her to get off her feet, so Vance helped her up and they went back upstairs. I got up, turned the lights off, and shook my head thinking and worrying about my sister and the baby.

Saturday morning I woke up to the sun peeking through my window. I heard the birds chirping away outside, hopefully telling me that it was going to be a lovely day. I looked at the clock and to my surprise; it was ten-thirty a.m. I must have been dog tired to have slept that long, it was truly out of character for me. Surprisingly, it was quiet in the house. It was real refreshing not to hear Vance and Sharise bickering. I figured maybe they had gone out to the store. I stepped into the shower and enjoyed the water washing yesterday's troubles from me. When I finished drying off, the familiar sounds of Sharise and Vance arguing was seeping through the door from downstairs. I starting hearing more of the familiar noises that I was used to. I couldn't believe his dumb ass was arguing with her after last night and the condition that she was in. Sharise voice was constantly accusing him of something, and he stood his ground on being clueless.

"I don't what you're talking about." It was getting louder, more than usual, so I got my clothes on and made it downstairs. It didn't take long for Vance to forget about the small tragedy we had last night. When I walked in the kitchen, Sharise was sitting at the table and Vance was leaning against the wall. "Well, are you gonna tell her or should I?" Vance asked Sharise.

Sharise looked up at him and said, "I told you that I would handle this, would you please let me?" Vance stormed out, telling

Sharise that she'd better or he would.

"What the fuck did he just say?" Sharise was trying to calm me down. "What is going on, Sharise? Are you still bleeding? Does your stomach feel okay?" She assured me that she hadn't seen any signs of blood that morning.

"I called the doctor and he told me to take it easy for a few days. He called it break through bleeding. The baby is just implanting itself in my uterus. The doctor told me to take off from work and take it easy for a few days," she told me.

I felt relieved. Then, I wondered what was the yelling about between the two of them. "Were you talking to you about the bills?" I asked her.

Sharise was hesitant and told me that she had to talk to me, sister to sister. I wondered was she going to talk to me about, maybe her thinking about Vance fucking around on her. She was a woman and my flesh and blood, and she probably felt the truth with her woman's intuition. And damn it, I felt it my duty as her sister to tell her if she asked about him fucking around when the time came. But, I didn't want any part of getting her upset, no matter how true it was. I still thought it is a right time and place for everything. It just was not the time. I sat down and was ready to make sense out of the madness of what was going on. She looked at me and told me that she and Vance simply could not pay the bills because they honestly had put their last bit of money inside the envelopes already.

"If you needed the money, Shante, why wouldn't you just say that instead of blaming Vance and I of stealing it." What the hell was that? Was that how the conversation was supposed to happen? I was bracing myself to tell her gently if need be about Vance being a no good motherfucker, but then all of a sudden I was the one being blamed and put in the middle of their private little hell. "Vance has told me of other things that have been going on while I haven't been home. I love you and you know that, but I could never share my man with you. Why are you putting all of this pressure on him? Are you that upset about not having a man in your life that you would stoop so low to be with Vance? Do you think that I wouldn't know?"

My eyes were filling up with water. I felt as though Sharise had punched me in the gut real good, and it hurt so badly. I felt as though I was in the *Twilight Zone*. I swallowed hard. "Sharise. Why?" I asked while crying. I could not believe that my own sister believed whatever that bastard had filled her head up with. They always said that blood was thicker than water, but right then I felt that saying was just a myth. That old saying was not applying to me. I went over to her and tried to console her with a hug, but she rejected me and didn't want me to touch her. I looked at my sister and tried to be delicate with what I was going to say. "Sharise, I love you. You are my only sister. First of all, I don't think that it would not be fair for me to pay all the utilities in this house. Why would I steal the money from the bills? I'm telling you the God given truth; I put my money in there. Somewhere along the way, that money was taken out and I believe it was Vance that took it. And, I would never try and take your man from you. I never had any feelings for Vance from day one. I have tolerated him in our home because of you." She started shaking and holding her stomach as though she was in pain. I ran over and told her that we should put all of this behind us. I didn't want her to lose her baby because of unnecessary stress. I had to bite my tongue real hard because I really wanted to tell her about that dog of a man she had, but I knew it wouldn't matter because at that point, she wouldn't believe me anyway so I helped her to the couch to lay down and rest. I went on the front porch and got the *Post* newspaper, then sat down and opened to the want ads. As painful as it was, I had to leave my home and find my own apartment.

By the end of the day, I had managed to write down ten apartments that I was going to check out the next day. All of them were not too far from my job and was conveniently on the bus line if I had to take it. I went downstairs to fix me a peanut butter and jelly sandwich, then went back upstairs and knocked on Sharise door before I went in my room.

"Sharise, do you need anything before I start reading my novel?"

She told me to come in. Vance had not gotten home yet and I went in and sat on the bed beside her. We started talking and it was such a nice conversation, just like old times. It was as though nothing had ever happened. We giggled as we brought up Ma and Da, and our sorrows from losing them was turning into joy as we reminisced about the good times with them. That moment was short lived as we heard the front door open. It was Vance. Sharise's entire attitude started to change and as much as I hated to, I took that opportunity to tell Sharise of my plans of moving out. She looked totally shocked, and I hoped she didn't think that I was doing it out of spite. I just couldn't live in those conditions anymore. I reached into my purse and gave her an envelope with four checks written out to all the utility companies. I did that out of the goodness of my heart, to help my sister and my future niece or nephew. I got up and walked out, passing Vance by in the hall without a saying a damn word.

It didn't take long for me to find a place. The Woodner was only the second place that I had visited and soon as I walked in, I loved everything about it. It was perfect. I wrote a check for the deposit with butterflies in my stomach. I was scared to death, but I prayed to God and asked Him to be with me in the decision that I was making.

My move in date was in two weeks. I thought about Sharise and hated to leave, but I could not stay in that house with Vance in there for another minute. I went home and broke the news to my sister. She couldn't believe that I was really going to leave. Vance, on the other hand, had nothing to say. I think he was rather glad that it worked out that way. He had a free ticket and his secret was never revealed about the backstabbing dog he was. But, if my sister's intuition kicked in, it would be a matter of time. On the other hand, he had to become responsible for Sharise and his baby, and start paying the bills for the household. There would be no one around to blame about missing money anymore, and I was not about to stay there and take care of the two of them with a baby.

My car was packed with the little stuff I had. I ran and hugged Sharise. "If you need me, just pick up the phone anytime to call. I'll be seeing you a lot, we only live thirty minutes from each other." I looked toward the porch and Vance put his beer up to me as though he was giving a toast.

"Take care of yourself out there girl."

"Yeah, I will. Vance, please be good to my sister."

"You know I will." I waved good bye to Vance as he stood on the porch with a beer in his hand. I pulled out of my park wiping tears from my eyes, looking in the rear view, and seeing the only home that I'd ever known. It was a new day and I had to live for myself.

CHAPTER SEVEN

Being Independent And In Love

Time had passed and I had gotten used to living by myself. I begin to mingle a lot more and got involved with a book club called Sisters of Literacy. The sky was the limit in our book club, we didn't have any restrictions on what we read. Every month, one member would suggest their book of choice and each of us would read and review it. At the meetings there were hot discussions because each member had their own personality.

De'nuiqa was a young girl from the hood who brought a lot of street smart views to our discussions on the piece of literature we were discussing at the time. She always gave her opinions and perspectives on topics we were discussing. Her personality was straight ghetto, but her opinions were interesting. Mi'juhnae, a step down from De'nuiqa, had a little less class and her opinions were a little grouchier than De'nuiqa. If a character was a slut in the book, she would just say, 'Hey she had to do what she had to do.' And there was Diamond, who was a constant bragger. I didn't know what it was about with her, but hello, we came to talk about the book, not her and what she had or planned to get. She had to be cut off in many conversations because of her getting off the subject and focusing on herself. She would start talking about a character from the book and would end up talking about her or what she had and how much it cost. She struck me as being very vain. There were six other members, including myself, who were ordinary members who just fit in with life.

Our first book was *G Spot* written by Noire. After I read that first book, I started reading Zane's famous diaries. After that, I was hooked, they became two of my favorite authors. They showed me through their writings that they were not afraid of what others thought. It may be shocking at first, but hey, like I said, they were not afraid. And because of that, they gave me courage to pursue my poetry a little more and one day let others hear me as being proud and not ashamed. Their books were hot and heavy. I would enjoy reading them, especially at night. I rated the books on how many batteries I would have to use for my electric toy. If the book was really good, I would turn my light off at night and let my imagination grow wild, farfetched in fantasy. I never inserted the toy, but just used it to sooth my swollen clit until I released my juices and my little pocketbook would close. After awhile, that grew tiresome and I hoped that I would meet someone someday soon. I wanted so badly for a man to love me and need me. I wanted to feel a real man that could hold me. And, I was dying to feel his muscle inside of me. I was twenty two and still a virgin, it was sad to me. I went to bed still thinking about my life, but soon sleep came and soothed my mind for the night.

Monday morning had arrived and my alarm was going off, reminding me that the weekend was over. I hit the snooze one more time, then finally got up and stretched my arms while letting out a yawn. It felt so good. I glanced at the calendar and saw that it was May first, with a big red circle around the thirty first of May, showing me that my birthday was coming up at the end of the month. I started thinking that soon I would be twenty three, alone, and yes, still a damn virgin. Oh well, I figured I would think positive for the rest of the day. Maybe something good would fall from the sky. I finally started to get dressed and ready for work. Spring was here and it was a beautiful day, so I decided to wear a tight mini skirt with a nice, sexy blouse. It was not too revealing, but it made a nigger wonder and want to see more. My pumps were three inches high. I went into my purse to get my lipstick, and put my favorite shade on, Velvet Crush. I looked myself over once again for approval, then left out, got into my car, and headed for my office to start my day.

On my way to the office, I was getting mad attention. Every guy that I passed that day seemed to notice me. I pulled up to the garage and showed my ID to Officer Jerry, who had been the security attendant there for awhile. Jerry was a handsome, tall guy in his mid forties. He was very courteous and sported a beautiful smile. He always knew how to give a compliment in a tasteful manner.

"Hey, good looking, you might need my assistance up in the office today. You're looking mighty nice, today. I may have to arrest a couple today. They just might get out of line when they see you today," he said while laughing. Jerry was funny. He let the vehicle control arm up and we laughed as I went into my parking space.

Everyone was in such a good mood for a Monday morning. When I got off the elevator, everyone I passed by put me in the spotlight. "Whew, hubba hubba," were the comments. "Has anybody seen Shante?" I got compliments walking all the way down to my office. That made me feel real good. But, on the other hand as I thought to myself, was I was looking like a bum on other days.

By noon, I had gotten swamped with work, but I was good at organizing my work with pressure and time constraints. I was so busy that I didn't realize there was a customer standing in front of the desk waiting to be helped. He cleared his throat to get my attention. When I looked up, I saw the finest tall drink of water I'd ever seen. Immediately, I became thirsty as hell and wanted to drink from his fountain. It was the day I had met the man of my dreams, Melvin Brenin, who later became my husband. I still remember the first time we laid eyes on each other. I never believed in love at first sight, but when we looked into each other's eyes, there was a spark that was ignited in the both of us. I immediately felt a connected to him. One of my duties at work was overseeing the supplies for the office and he wanted to bid on the contract. Technically, any company that I chose had to have a great reputation. I would have to check their credit record, other jobs that the company might have worked for in the past, but when I laid eyes on him, I just knew he was going to get the contract, and maybe a little more, like me, perhaps. As I looked down at his hand for a ring and I didn't see one, I hoped that he didn't forget it at home and he just didn't have it on. While I handled all of his paperwork, I pretended to take him through all the steps. He sat down and filled out everything, and while he did that, we talked. He told me that he had just moved in a house located in Silver Spring, Maryland and I told him that I was in College Park, Maryland, in a one bedroom apartment. We laughed and talked for two hours and before we knew it, it was lunch time. Melvin suggested that we go grab a bite to eat and I agreed, so we left out with all eyes on us. Of course, I let him have the contract to supply us with office supplies twice a month.

Every time he came to the office, our attraction grew stronger for one another. On the days he made deliveries, I made sure I would dress for the occasion. Each time, my dress would get more revealing to attract him even more. It was funny how we ladies go after what we want. Like a black widow spider, sometimes we weren't that different. We go through a lot to attract our prey, captivate him with all our beauty. Then trap him in our web because he wants it, then bang, we got him. The difference with me was I didn't want to kill and eat him, I just wanted to get him and love him.

CHAPTER EIGHT

Not A Virgin Anymore

Melvin and I started going out and we became a hot item. I met his friends and he wanted me to meet his family. He invited me to a barbeque at his parent's house on the weekend, which was my birthday. I was trying to think of something to do, so I guess that would suffice. So, for my birthday, I was going to with meet Melvin's family.

The day had finally arrived. I woke up to my 23rd Birthday and yelled out, "Happy birthday to me!" I climbed out of bed, got on my knees, and thanked God for another year on my life. Ma and Da had raised me and Sharise with that tradition. The phone rang and it was Sharise wishing me a happy birthday. We talked and I asked her about her fourth baby. She was due at any minute and Sharise told me that she was so ready to go. I asked how Vance was doing and she got quiet, so I knew something was wrong. Finally, she blurted out that things were good, and then Sharise told me that she was going to quit her job.

"Don't worry, Vance got a better job and is making much more money, so we are doing well." I still had no idea what he did, but I took her word for it, then hung up the phone.

I jumped up and started looking for something to impress Melvin's family. Since it was just a barbeque, I figured that I would wear some nice jeans. The phone rang and I answered.

"Hello, baby, it's me, your intensified, bonafide lover." Melvin was something at times.

"Why do you say the things that you do? You know we are not in that stage yet." I was smiling from ear to ear. "I told you I want to wait until things are much more serious for things like that."

Melvin sighed. "You know, baby, you are living in the Stone Age. Even though I know it's been only a month, I know you are the one for me. Once I feed you like a baby, the time we've been together won't even matter to you anymore. I can make things so intense for you; this traditional time thing will be of the past. There are no rules with me, baby." Melvin made me lose my mind when I talked to him, so I told him that I would see him when he picked me up. We hung up and it had just dawned on me that he did not wish me a happy birthday.

I put on my jeans with my nice, cool top, not revealing too much because it was time to impress. It was twelve noon and my doorbell rang. My hands were getting sweaty, and my heart had started beating fast. I wiped my hands along the sides of my hips and opened the door. To my surprise, it was not Melvin, but a delivery of the most beautiful flowers and balloons that had been sent to me. I couldn't wait to get to the card. It read, *Happy Birthday. P.S. You have made me happier in the past four weeks than anybody ever has. I will return the favor. I promise you that.* I couldn't get the smile off my face. Shortly after, the doorbell rang again and it was Melvin. He said happy birthday, grabbed me around my waist, and smothered my lips with the most sensual kiss. Something went through my body and I was more in love with him in just that short amount of time.

We pulled up in an area which was known as the gold coast off of 16th Street. It was an exclusive area where a lot of doctors, lawyers, and professional people lived. The houses were gorgeous. He pulled up in a long drive way and there were seven cars already parked. My heart had started beating fast, I was really getting nervous. He told me to hold tight, and he got out and came around to open my door. He grabbed my hand and told me that it would be okay and not to be nervous.

"Be yourself, they are going to love you." He kissed me again and we stepped in the house.

The barbeque smelled real good and the music was pumping from the backyard. We walked through the house to get to the back. While passing in the kitchen, a young girl screaming Melvin's name and rushed over to hug him. "I'm glad you came." She looked over at me. "You must be Shante. He has been raving about you, girl, ever since he met you. I'm Melvin's sister, Bridgett." Bridgett seemed to be around the age of sixteen. She was spunky free spirited with a big smile. "I'm so happy that he found someone to put up with his crazy butt." We started laughing and I instantly felt welcomed.

Bridgett grabbed my hand and took me out back to meet everyone. All of Melvin's family was so nice and down to earth. His parents were very classy and not stuck up at all. Melvin introduced me to his brother, David, who was acting very odd. He greeted me, but he didn't talk to me like everyone else, he just kept staring at me from the other corner of the basement. It seemed as though he was in seclusion from everyone else. For most of the evening, he stayed to himself and kept staring at me. At one point during the evening, all of us women were having a good conversation and I looked over in the corner and Melvin and David seemed to be having a heated conversation about something.

"Are you sure?" was all I could make out of the discussion they were having. David turned and saw me staring at him, and then he nodded his head at me then left. He didn't say goodbye to anybody and I felt like something was wrong. We all sat around laughing and talking until ten that night. I was so glad that I had met everyone. When we got our fill on the delicious food, it was time to go. I thanked everyone for having me over, then we left to go home.

I could tell that something was on Melvin's mind the entire ride home, but I didn't ask him about anything. When we finally arrived in front of my place, Melvin got out and opened my door. He gave me a good night kiss and walked me to the front door to make sure that I was safely inside. When he turned to leave, I stopped him.

"Melvin, can you please stay and give me a much deserved birthday present?" I couldn't believe that I was being so forward, but hell, it was my birthday.

Sparks flew and he closed and locked the door. I went to the couch and waited for him. Melvin came to me and started caressing me, and it felt so good. He planted a passionate kiss upon my lips, diving into my mouth and exploring me with his tongue. I could not believe what was happening, it shocked me but it felt good, so I didn't pull away. He looked at me.

"Are you sure about this?"

I told him, "Yes, I am."

Melvin lay on top of me and I felt his huge bulge rising between us and it was huger than I had expected. The only one of those that I knew about was when I caught Vance and Sharise. I read about it in the books so many times, but it was my first in real life. Melvin got up and took my hand, pulling me up and taking me to my bedroom. I was getting nervous, but I completely trusted him. He quickly eased my concerns by just holding me tight against him. He led me to the bed while at the same time, lacing me down with his sensual, savory kisses. He then started slipping me out of my clothes, taking my blouse off, and then he unzipped my jeans. I lift my leg to release it free and then the other came out of the jeans. He let my breast out and started kissing, caressing, and sucking each one. It felt amazing to me. Melvin's finger caressed the brim of my panties, making me shiver with desire. He looked at me and asked me did I want him to take them off. He taunted me over and over, asking me was I sure that he could see my goodies.

I whispered, "Yes," shyly to him.

He moaned as he slowly pulled my panties down. "Damn, baby, you are so beautiful." He grunted. I started unbuttoning his shirt, revealing his masculine chest as I gently kissed it. He took my hand and led it to his pants buckle to undo them. He took my hand and placed it on his stiff manhood. "Rub it, baby, don't be afraid. Rub it and make me feel good."

I felt awkward because I didn't know what I was doing. He detected that so he started guided my hands with the motion. He moaned, "Yeah, that's it, baby, that feels real good." He got up and pulled off his underwear. I started freezing up again at the sight of his naked, masculine body with a fully erected rod standing straight at attention. He got in the bed and told me to trust him. "This will be the best thing you have ever had. I promise." Melvin fingered me to get me ready. It shocked me at first, but damn, it was feeling good. He got me going to his motion, first slow, and then fast, he was about to make me go crazy. He looked into my eyes and asked me was I ready.

"Yes," I moaned with desire.

He spread my legs further and started guided himself in. Melvin had made me so wet that it was no pain, only pleasure. He plunged into me with such sweetness; I swear I felt like I heard the damn orchestra playing outside the window to our lovemaking. I started to feel something building up within my walls, and it wanted to explode every time Melvin hit it. It felt like built up pressure with trebles of pulsating muscles deep within my pussy. It got more intense every time he touched it. I wanted to scream, but I just moaned.

Melvin looked at me and said, "Baby, I can feel you're getting ready to pop," so he stroked me slower. He told me to hold it.

"I can't." Breathing heavily, I tried to grind up to him to get the motion going again. He stopped moving within me and told me to slow down the pace.

"Relax, baby, I don't want to cum yet." I guess I was acting like sexed crazed fiend. Even though it was my first time, I was real hungry for it. Melvin started the motion again. He placed his finger on my clit and started rubbing it. I wasn't able to control anything anymore. That feeling came back each time he hit my spot.

"Please, Melvin, I want to explode." He told me to hold it. It was so intense and I couldn't go on, so I let myself go. It seemed to be an eruption of wetness and at the same time, Melvin came with me. He had timed it perfectly, we came together, and that was just beautiful. I fell asleep in his arms.

When morning came, Melvin was gone, but he left a rose from the collection he gave me on the pillow next to me. It was such a sweet gesture from such a sweet guy.

Melvin was due to come in at seven that morning for an early delivery. I made to dress sexy for him. I got in the shower, getting hot every time I got a flash back of the night's events. The hot water felt good as it hit my skin and I closed my eyes as I used the sponge to go across my breast, imagining it being Melvin as I leaned under the hot, steamy water, tantalizing my skin with every drop that hit it. My sponge had made its way between my legs where I hoped Melvin would be again soon. I started to rub back and forth, getting into a nice, gentle pattern and was startled when I heard a loud bang. I dropped my soap. My eyes opened and I looked around to find my soap had feel from the soap holder in the shower. That took me out of the mood, and I hurried to get to work.

I heard the elevator arrive and open as I was at my desk crunching some numbers for an account. I knew it was Melvin, I could feel his presence. As soon as I started thinking about him, he walked into my office with that gorgeous smile of his. I immediately met him with mine and we were once again connected. We were definitely attracted to each other, it was how I knew he was the one.

Melvin came in with an order of supplies that I had placed with his company. He gave me the invoice to look over and double check. Once I signed my signature, I got up and took Melvin to the supply room. We had to walk by many of my co workers with big smiles on their faces. They teased by giving the goo eyes and making little gestures. I just smiled and continued on past their desk. I unlocked the door and once inside, Melvin took off his jacket and exposed his golden biceps. I hope it wasn't obvious that I was gawking, but damn it, I was. The way his body flexed and the way he handled those boxes, it reminded me of his handling of me the night before. I started sweating, so I grabbed a piece of cardboard and started fanning. He looked over at me laughing.

"It is hot in here, huh?"

I shook my head agreeing. "Yeah."

I stood mesmerized as he neatly stacked the products on the shelves. His physic was to die for. Melvin finally finished and we started to leave out. I reached for the knob, and suddenly felt a slap on my rear that he had just given me. I didn't turn around immediately because I was blushing so hard. I barely opened the door before Melvin reached from behind me and gently pushed the door close. He turned me around, pulled me close to him, and planted a kiss on my lips.

"That was an anchor for letting me explore what's mine last night." I smiled and blushed.

After that encounter, along with the previous night, the deal was sealed. We belonged to each other. Melvin left and I went back to my desk, not getting any work done that day because of my daydreaming.

CHAPTER NINE

Present Day, Back In Focus

My mind slipped away from the reminiscing of the past and I was brought back into the present by my computer telling me, 'You've got mail.' I turned around from the window and saw the mail image dancing around on my screen. I clicked on it and saw it was from my best friend, Terrance. *Do you want to meet me at the bistro on fifth and Nate for lunch?* I started smiling from ear to ear. As I sat there, it was only another minute until my phone started ringing. I picked up, answering, "Dave and Donavan Associates, Shante Brenin speaking."

There was a hesitation, and then a male voice responded, "Yes, Mrs. Shante Brenin, this is a courtesy call from the Lexus Car dealership in Annapolis, Maryland. I am calling to ask you about your payment this month. We have not received it." I was shocked and could not believe a bill collector was calling me, but through the silence on the phone I started to hear a snicker and I heard Terrance's voice. "What's up, girl. Look, stop showing all of them pearly whites of yours." He knew that I was cheesing.

Terrance always knew what to say when he wanted to break my concentration. We had been best friends ever since we had graduated from high school. We talked every day we could. It was amazing that we shared everything together except one thing, and that was being physical with each other. I knew that if anybody ever heard me say that about Terrance, they would say that they had suspected us two all along of having an affair. I was a married woman and to most people the term best friend, in my case, should be my husband. I loved my husband and we had a close bond, but I had a different kind of bond with Terrance. I knew not one person would understand what I was trying to say, and that's why I rarely mentioned Terrance to anybody because it seemed that society had already made up its mind about a married women and her best guy friend. We had been convicted of an affair that had never happened and to play it safe, we were careful not to display the flauntiest of playful actions that we sometimes had with each other. We knew each other and that was all that mattered.

The Bistro was a nice, cozy place that served the best food and gave you entertainment in the form of poetry readings at the same time. I loved to go there and hear each poet bare their souls. Sometimes, you could feel their joy, sorrows, love, or happiness. Friday nights it was amateur night. I promised myself that one night I would have the courage to participate, and read and share my feelings with others, unleash what was bottled up inside me. When it came down to it, fear was a factor that held me back. Even though many years had passed since Mr. Hayes, my algebra teacher, had embarrassed and humiliated me, I still felt like he is standing over me, reading the intimate lines that I had written. Deep down, I knew that only time would tell.

I told Terrace that I would meet him at the Bistro at twelve. As I hung up with a chuckle and grin on my face, I looked up at Greg, a co worker, standing in my doorway with a conniving grin on his face. I didn't know how long he had been standing there, but his eyes told me that he had been standing there long enough to irritate me.

"Well, can I come for lunch, too?" Greg asked. My grin immediately turned upside down. "Well, that was your husband, right? I like the bistro, can I cooooome? Or, will it be enough of that going on?"

I could not stand Greg most of the time. I didn't know why he was like he was, but on second thought, I did know. Everyone in the office knew of his tendencies. He had nothing but feminist ways about him, and he also had his time of months. He was nosy as hell and loved to get in your business when he could. And, don't let him get a wind of anything that you were doing because he was sure to spread it around like butter. He would never get the facts on something, if it was juicy, that's how he was going to carry it. While Greg stood there waiting, my phone rang. I got up and told Greg to excuse me, then politely closed the door in his face. I ran and answered the phone.

"Dave and Donovan Associates, Shante Brenin speaking, how I can help you?"

On the other end someone was sobbing and called my name

out. "Shante, he, he awwwww." I looked at my caller ID and it was my sister.

"Sharise, what's wrong? Calm down and tell me what's wrong." She took a few minutes, and then started talking a little clearer with an occasional sob. I asked her was she hurt, and then I asked her about my nieces and nephews. "Are the kids okay?"

As soon as she had the first one, she quit her job at AT&T and said that Vance was going to take care of her and the kids, Brandon, Troy, and Monique. She had them back to back. I occasionally carried a chip on my shoulder about the house that belonged to my sister and I. It just burned me up that I gave my house up all because of….. Just thinking about it gave me such a headache. But, when I thought of those innocent kids, I tried to put it behind me because I knew that they could not help themselves. I loved them very much, as though they were my own. I sacrificed and never said a word to Sharise about it. She stayed at home and Vance was doing whatever it was he did. I remember the day when she went for her six week check up after having Brandon, and the doctor gave her their news that she was expecting again. She called me and cried like a baby. Lord, I guess Vance just couldn't wait. I wasn't surprised.

She assured me that everyone was alright, I asked her about her well being. "Is everything alright with you? Are you feeling okay?" Then, I asked about Vance. When I asked about him she started to sniffle again, so I knew he was the root of the problem. It was silent on the phone for about three minutes.

Finally, Sharise broke her silence and said, "Shante, I think that Vance is messing around on me."

I was a little stunned, but it didn't seem like news to me. It just brought back memories of the many times I had to ward off his advances toward me when I was younger. I had to meet Terrance in five minutes, so I told Sharise that I was sure that everything was going to be alright, and I told her that I would call her back as soon as I got back from lunch. Sharise hesitated on the phone and did not want to hang up.

"Sharise, honey, I'm telling you, I think that it's going to be alright," I told her.

"No, Shante, please listen to me," she pleaded. The conversation was very strange. I couldn't make out what she was talking about. I asked her had he confessed to anything and Sharise started crying again. She told me that she had evidence.

"What have you found?" I asked her while looking at my watch. I was already ten minutes late for meeting Terrace at the Bistro. I didn't want to seem insensitive to my sister, but she went through the charade every other week. I knew I was not Dr. Phil or anything, but it was plain as anything that Vance was out there sleeping around all the late nights he should have been home from work. "I'm thinking about all the hang ups and the match books from the clubs and hotels in his coat pockets. Sharise began telling me more, and then my cell phone rang. I looked and it was Terrance. I had to interrupt my sister and told her that I had an important meeting that I was late for. "Look, Sharise, I will have to call you back in about two hours," I told her. I hung up from Sharise, and then answered my cell as I stood up grabbing my keys and walking out of the office, closing the door behind me. "Hey, I'm on my way," I told Terrance.

He responded with his humor as usual. "Man, I'm dying of hunger over here waiting."

I told him to hold on, just give me five minutes. I hung up and was off briskly, walking down the hall making my way to the elevator.

CHAPTER TEN

A Friendship That Will Last Forever

I pushed the down button on the wall and patiently waited. I hoped no one would come and share the elevator with me, but no such luck because I heard footsteps coming around the corner toward me. As the footsteps became closer, I pushed the button more intensely, hoping that the doors would swing open in time for me to jump in, push the close button, and be on my way. But, the footsteps coming around the corner got closer and closer, and stopped beside me. When I looked up, Greg was standing beside me with a sinister grin on his faced.

"Okay, honey, I'm ready for our lunch date. Where are you taking me?" Greg asked. Before I responded, the elevator doors finally opened up and we both stepped in. Greg pushed the third floor and I pushed the garage level.

I looked at Greg and asked, "Oh, wouldn't you like to know?"

We arrived at the third floor, Greg got out, he waved goodbye, and left out. I guess I could stand Greg for a minute as a co worker, but sometimes things could get so irritating when he was around. Greg thought he knew everything and like I said before, he never got the facts straight before he ran off with his version of the news. He had some good qualities about him, like he dressed his ass off every day. Everything matched from his head to his feet. He smelled nice every day, too. But, we also shared one similarity, Greg loved men. It was not a secret and he didn't care, it was just Greg being Greg. It was his preference, to each his own.

The button for the garage was lit up and I walked out. I passed by Jerry. "It's time for lunch already?" He had his charming smile still across his face. I must say that Jerry was the only security guard that acted as though he had any sense. Sometimes, it made one wonder if any of those sexual harassment classes that security guards were required to take did any good. I knew that Jerry was a keeper. He definitely was the most admirable guard there. He waved while I raced to my Lexus, unlocked the door, and got in; finally I was on my way. While driving down the avenue my cell phone rang, so I pulled over and answered. There were strict driving laws in effect in the city. One of them included no driving while talking on the cell phone. If caught, you could get a one hundred dollar fine. I never wanted to risk it, so I would just pull over and talked. I went behind a parked car on the corner of the avenue of Tuckerman. I looked at my blinking phone and saw that it was Terrance. I pushed the talk button and answered.

"Yeah, well if it isn't, what is your name is again?" he asked.

"Okay, okay, I'm on my way, give me five minutes. I can't believe you called me off the road. I told you I was coming." I hung up, put my car in drive, and was off to meet my bud.

As I pulled up in front of Charlie's Bistro, the valet came to retrieve my keys. He was a real gentleman. I placed my hand out and he helped me up out of the car. I spotted Terrace sitting in the rear at the last table. I walked past Sweet Tea, a local jazz band that was playing a sexy sultry piece for a well known local poetess, Saundra D. She wore a long, flowing dress and was romancing the microphone as she recited her piece. I knew he wasn't mad, but he would like me to think that he was just to hear me beg for forgiveness. It was something we did in our friendship just for giggles. As I got closer to Terrace, he slightly turned toward me, recognizing the taps of my heels. I saw his cheeks getting high from the side and I knew he was happy that his buddy had arrived. He may have been a little pissed from waiting an extra fifteen minutes, but all that was under the rug now.

He turned around and had a mean face on. "Why in the hell you got to have a brother waiting on your slow ass?" he asked.

"Oh, I'm sorry about that, baby, let me make up to you," I playfully went along.

"How?" he asked while raising his eyebrows.

I sat down across from him, grabbed his hand, and seductively said, "First, I will order everything I like, then I will devour it because I'm real hungry. Then, when I'm finished, baby, I'll pay the check." We both burst out in laughter.

Terrance finally said, "Now I can roll with that. Girl, you are crazy, but still you're still my buddy, so I gotta love ya." The waiter came and handed us our menus, told us the fresh catch of the day, then took our drink orders. I ordered a glass of red wine and Terrance had a beer. He gave us a few minutes to look over the menu. I decided on the salmon that was served over a rice pilaf, and Terrace went with the same thing. Our waiter came back with our drinks and a hot basket of freshly made rolls. He took our orders and told us that it would be about ten minutes. The jazz number was so sultry that it relaxed me totally. On stage, Saundra wrapped her hands around the microphone seductively and started her piece.

I am held deep within your soul
I am a multitude of things
Yet invisible
Not showing myself until released
Your mind controls my being
I am a heat ray soothed by a breeze
I am the sun that settles in the evening
I am a tooth being extracted
From pounding nerves
I am a radiator being bled of steam
I am a dry throat being quenched from thirst
Despite all the tensions that I represent
I'll let you see colors
The prettiest rainbow in your mind
The brightest that was ever revealed
In the sky of your imagination
I control the ocean waves deep within you
I represent you fully and whole
I am the orgasm of life

She captivated the audience with that piece. It was so deep. Everyone gave her a great applause. Before Saundra D left, she announced about a poetry reading that was coming up in next month. "This will be an open mic event, so bring your talent to the stage.

Terrace turned to me. "That will be the perfect time for you to shine and read some of the things you have been writing. I would love to hear what you got on your mind."

I told him to forget about it because I could never be as good as those people. "Didn't you hear Saundra?"

Terrance told me that he thought in due time I would be just as good as her. "I think that a true poet has to probably live through some things." Terrace was the only one that I had ever let hear some of my old poetry. He always told me that it was nice and gave me so much encouragement with anything that I ever thought about. It stimulated my mind, and he kept doing it to try and make me act on some of my thoughts. Only a true friend would do that. That was why I felt so lucky to have him.

The jazz tunes had continued and our food had arrived. We started unraveling and unloading our troubles and joys of the day thus far with each other. My story started with me telling him about my day with Greg. Terrance listened, laughed, and made jokes about Greg. Even though he had never met him, he was so good at listening to all the details and sketched him out perfectly. He had me laughing so hard tears streamed from the corner of my eyes. Then, Terrance started telling me about a girl he had met last week at the bowling alley.

"Her name is Vanessa. She works for a lawyer's office downtown," he told me.

He had so much excitement in his voice. I was always happy for him when he had found someone special. He raved about a new girl so many times before. Each time I kept my fingers crossed, hoping that this would be the one for him so he would feel the special bond like Melvin and I felt with each other in our marital bliss. He seemed to be always looking for something special in someone. He always thought he had found the right one, but something always happened to disappoint him. I wanted him to feel special and feel the wonderful things with a significant other. My cell rang, and I looked down and saw it was Melvin. I excused myself from my conversation with Terrance, holding my finger up to him.

I pushed my talk button and answered, "Hey, baby."

He chuckled and said, "Hey, luscious. I hope I'm not interrupting anything. Are we still on for tonight for dinner and a movie?" I told him yeah, I had been thinking about it all day. He told me he loved me and then we hung up.

Terrance looked at me and playfully acted as though he was taking the phone away from me. The waiter came back and asked about a second drink. I told him no because I knew I had to go back to work, but Terrance started persuading me to have another one with him.

"Come on, Shante. What harm will it do? It's only one drink to relax you for the rest of the day." Like I said before, Terrace was quite the persuader. He was always so good at that. He made everything in life look like you never had to give a second thought.

Our second drinks arrived I looked at Terrance and said, "You know, Terrance, I don't know why I let you convince me into these things."

He looked at me and said, "Look, don't be wondering, just go and relax so you can go back to work and talk to your co worker in a nice manner, or curse his ass out if you wish."

We finished our lunch off with some much needed laughter. Terrance paid the bill and we got up and went up front to wait for our cars. The valet pulled up with our cars, and while we were waving our goodbyes, Terrance turned back around and yelled, "Hey, I'm serious, you need to get on that stage and let everybody know what you feel. Okay?" We waved goodbyes and snapped back into reality of going back to work, because lunch was over.

CHAPTER ELEVEN

Office Politics

I found myself once again looking out of my window as though I had nothing to do. The ringing of the phone snapped me back into reality. I answered and it was Melvin. "Hey, how is my honey bun?" Melvin asked.

I smiled, feeling warmed over with his sexy, sensual voice. "Fine," I replied. I loved Melvin so much.

"I've got something special for you tonight," he told me.

"What might that be, baby?" I asked him.

"Aw, aw. You will find out in due time." He told me that he would see me later, and then hung up.

I guess Melvin wanted to stay in instead of our original plans to go out. He had me in so much wonder. My mind drifted off to a couple of nights ago when he gazed into my eyes at the dinner table. We were having a steak dinner that I had surprised him with, and we had a debatable conversation on men and women; who were the most sensitive ones when it came to making love. I told him that it had to be women because I felt women were more in tuned to their surroundings, and men's first thoughts would be how they could be feeling after the ultimate goal was met. Our conversation had winded down and Melvin continually looked at me seductively. His eyes were burning a hole through my clothes. I smiled at him and started clearing the table. Melvin grabbed me around my waist, pulled me to him, and placed his mouth on mine, unleashing his tongue, plunging deep into my mouth. We both moaned with equally wanting pleasures. He reached down, messaging and cupping my breast. Every time he undid a button on my blouse, he kissed the next button away. I thought Melvin was trying to prove a point with our debate we had on women being more sensitive with feelings when making love. At the moment, I didn't care because it was feeling way too good. I lost my thoughts on where I stood in the argument because my thoughts were only focused on what was happening. And, that was all good. As usual, my thoughts were interrupted by something. This time, it was the company's new manager, Ms. Susan Downing, walking through my door.

She had been with our company for about a year and a half she was a young, slender, tall white woman with red hair with very strange and eccentric ways. She wore all kinds of crazy colors that never matched, along with a pair of earrings that never matched as well. She would follow with a pair of shoes that were different colors. I guess she wanted to be remembered for the trait. I couldn't figure it out.

Mr. Harris, the one that started the business was a very fair and generous man from Kentucky. Many people on first impressions would have thought he was a racist just from looking at him, but he was just the opposite. Mr. Harris was a kind gentleman who treated everyone fairly regardless of your race, color, or creed. He gave so much for his employees, and that made everyone give their best for him. We could have never asked for a nicer boss. But, nice things didn't always last because Mr. Harris left our branch to open up in another state. He would pop up every now and then, but he placed someone in his place to run the branch. I knew I could have done the job, but things didn't always go the way you wanted. So, that's how Susan entered my life.

I had been with the company for a while. I was there when the company was fresh and new, just beginning to grow. When I was promoted, I handled all of the company's clients' accounts. I had my own office and was pretty good at my job. I loved it until she came along. The harmony that we all used to know was a thing of the past. She came to the company, it seemed, to prove something. She wanted everyone to know that she was not to be messed with. She came in demanding respect, but with me, I felt that you had to give respect in order to receive respect. Susan was on a real big power trip but what really killed me about some people in positions like hers was they know nothing about what they were doing. She had no people skills whatsoever. Every time she got in a jam, she came to me for answers, and then would later feed it into one of the meetings. Their end result was that she would get all of the credit. I would hate to help her sometimes because I always felt that her job really belonged to me. I should have been placed there. But, my Da always raised me to treat people the way I would want to be treated. I had to pray on that all the time, and hoped that my sanity would remain stable and not allow me to one day go off on her and kick her ass, and leave me hopeless and without a job. God help me.

Susan entered my office with two big folders of accounts from fifty different companies that we dealt with, and placed them down on my desk. She didn't say good evening, hello, or even a simple hi. "These accounts need to be entered into a new system that I have created for easier record pull ups. I will need you to enter these into the system."

I looked at her without even looking at the work and said, "Good evening, Susan."

She looked at the work, still not at me as a person, and said, "Hello," as though she was talking to the folders she just put down.

She avoided me much as possible. Most of our communication was done through emails or the phone. I was thinking it was a small tragedy because I would be getting off in two hours and I would never finish all of the data entry unless I stayed on overtime, and I knew that would not be happening that afternoon. Susan was attempting to leave out without any response from me whatsoever. Before she got out of my door, I called her.

"Susan, why did you wait so late in the evening for me to enter these accounts into the system? This would take at least a day to set up," I told her.

Susan turned around and finally gave a little eye contact. "I did not receive these from the corporate office until after lunch. This is what your job consist of at times. You should be expecting more workloads like this in the near future. I need those done by tomorrow morning, nine o' clock on my desk." She then left, closing the door behind her.

That bitch. What made her think that I wanted to do her books all night? At that moment, I felt like the rest of my working day was going to be all hell after that. I had to get through it, gritting my teeth together every time I thought about Susan.

I replaced my thoughts with Melvin. I was real excited about the evening, but I guess that was out the window. Looking at those heavy, thick books, I would have to do an extra hour and take them home with me. I could work from my laptop at home. It was going to take me just about all night for this one. I turned to the computer and pulled up the new program. It took me about a half hour just to read through the new system and its many functions. Once I read through the program, I was ready to input. And hour had gone by and I was just getting to input the records. I only had thirty minutes left before my official time to sign out and go home. I began to gather my things that I would need to take home with me. I kept thinking it was no way that I would have time to put input everything and still have time for the evening that I was so anticipating with Melvin. I had a battle going on in my head, work versus pleasure. What to do, what to do?

As I was packing my things, Greg slithered through my door and sat down. "Well, I hear you had a visit from Santa giving you lots of goodies to take home," Greg bellowed. I rolled my eyes because I knew the town crier was ready to give or receive some new gossip. He looked on my desk and touched the two books that I would be working from. "My, what big books you have. Are these your goodies?" Greg asked with a grin. I ignored him and asked him what he wanted. I really was not in the mood for him at the moment. He looked around to see if anyone would hear him. It was his classic move before giving his big gossip. "Well, I hear that Susan is trying to clean house in this office. I think she wants to fill this office with more friendly based people, say like her friends or maybe some family. She has to do it in a slick and discreet way of course. Susan probably is planning on getting rid of who she wants one by one. Or, only the ones that she thinks is dead weight. Not that you don't produce, but if she had something on you, or she may even try to make something on you. What are these books for?"

I told Greg that Susan wanted them imputed. "I don't know why this information should be put in this system, it needed a more updated version, but she is the boss."

Greg touched the books and said, "Well, this may be one of her ways." He gave me a tissue and I asked Greg what is was for. He left out saying, "Never let her see you sweat, darling."

I looked at the accountant books and wondered where I went wrong in my life. Things really should have been different for me. I thought about how I was going to go away to college, but chose the path straight into the working world. What was I thinking? I guess Mr. Harris made the place so nice for everyone that I was comfortable, only living in that day, never thinking about the future. Things would be a lot different if I held that position. I would never be a power tripping woman that had to be the head of everything. Second, I would never treat people as though they really didn't matter. I sat down at my desk, opened the drawer, and noticed a folded piece of paper that I had put away when I first started working there. I pulled it out, opened it, and saw those two lines that I had written so long ago.

A satisfied Black woman
Will I ever know?

I started thinking about the feeling I got earlier at the Bistro. The words flowed so smoothly from that poet. Her words had so much feeling and truth; it was amazing to me how her words just poured from her soul. I felt that I could do the same when I saw those lines that I had written. Those lines reflected my life at the time and I wanted others to know what was feeling. Honestly, thinking about my life, I still didn't have the answer to that question. I stared again out of the window, turned back to the desk, and wrote underneath those lines:

A lifetime of thinking and wondering
Which way I should really go

Those next lines came easy to me, and I liked them, I was really feeling them. I folded the paper, put in my purse, gathered my things, including those two big accountant books, closed and locked my door, and walked down the hall toward the elevator. As I passed Susan's office, she was sitting at her desk talking to someone. I thought she was on the phone, but as I passed by it was Greg. I said to myself, *Gee, that Greg sure gets around.* I was not going to worry about it, besides, he was her secretary. He had to work in close quarters with her. As I got to the end of the hall I heard friendly laughter. That never flies right with a sister when you have just passed people and you got laughter. It would always put distrust in your heart and your mind started to wonder about what had just been said. Were they in there discussing an employee's fate? I tried to dismiss my thoughts about it but my suspicions would not leave me alone. My elevator was there as soon as I pushed the button. I was so relieved that it was Thursday and I only had one more day to go.

CHAPTER TWELVE

Still Steamy And Hot

The drive home was not as relaxing as it usually was. All I could think of going home was how my day was the minute that Susan stepped in my office with her demands. I had not figured what it was about the small friction we had between each other, and of course, I couldn't get Greg's two cents on the situation either. I was a hell of a worker and I was very good at my job, but with her after my job, I had to really watch my back. I popped in my favorite jazz CD while trying to relax my mind as the sweet saxophone sounds went into my soul and started soothing me.

I finally made it home, pulling alongside Melvin's car in the driveway, feeling grateful that he was there. I had a lot of lonely moments at home because of his profession. He was the regional supplier which kept him traveling a lot. Sometimes, I wished we had a child to help fill the void when he was not there. I put the key in the door, and Melvin came and greeted me with a kiss. He grabbed my purse and the accountant books from my hand and placed them down on the floor. He had some mellow music going on from the oldies collection. Keith Sweat was singing *Make It Last Forever*. I looked toward the bedroom wall and saw shadows from the flickering of the candles he had lit to set the scene for me. Melvin forcefully pulled me toward him and powerfully kissed me and told me he had been thinking about me all day. It didn't take long before for my juices started flowing. He took me way off guard from the moment I stepped into the house. He started undoing my blouse, exposing my lace bra which he took no time to let my breast free from the bondage they were held in all day.

He whispered in my ear, "I've been thinking of you all day." I touched his masculine, thick muscles. He lifted my skirt, and reached for my lace panties and ripped them off. That sent a wave of excitement within me, making my pussy immediately wet for him. We swayed to the music with our bodies. The next tune came on with Luther singing *If Only for One Night*. Melvin dropped to his knees, spreading my legs apart as he looked up at me. He dipped his finger in my wetness, making me moan with pleasure. Melvin moaned, "I can't wait to taste you." He licked his finger and sucked it sensually. "Delectably yummy. Damn, girl, you taste good."

He started kissing my thighs, moving closer to my joy box. He kissed up one to the other simultaneously until he was in the center of my pleasure. He spread my lips open and started to lick every fold that he could find. He found folds that I didn't even know I had. My mind raced in full throttle as he played with my pearl, making it swell to unknown sizes and dimensions. I told him that I was about to reach my high on that highest mountain top. He then abruptly stopped, which made me want to whimper and cry like a baby from the withdrawal of the bottle. He stood up and put his fingers to my lips. "Shh, baby, I have so much more for you."

Melvin caressed and kissed my nipples. I undid his pants and reached down to find my stiff reward waiting to be released. I reached in and pulled out my awaiting prize fully erected just for me. He moaned as I got down giving him the feel of my tongue wrapped around his velvet rod of pleasure. He pulled me up because it would not take him long to explode within the wetness of my mouth. He took me to the couch and opened my legs, exposing my swollen lips that really needed to be relieved of the built up pressure. He massaged me there and then started to taunt me. Melvin looked up and me and asked, "Baby, tell me what you want right now?" He cupped and massaged me between my legs so passionately I thought I was going to die. He slipped a finger inside of me and began to make me go with his rhythm. I thought I was going to lose my mind. I could not take it any longer.

"Melvin, please stop and give me what I need," I pleaded. He was ready for him to slip into me but he waited. He started stroking his finger faster into me. I was about to explode, but I wanted every inch of him inside of me. "Please, Melvin, go inside and fuck me now," I screamed.

That's all he wanted to hear me say. He didn't hesitate another minute. Before I knew it, Melvin had entered me, not forcefully, but lovingly. He slid in with such ease and filled me completely. We went with each other's rhythm perfectly; Melvin's breathing became harder as his strokes became more profound in my pussy as he found my spot.

"Yes, that's it, baby." I finally gave up all eruptions that were pent up in me for so long. Melvin came right behind me with a loud roar. We collapsed, holding each other.

We smiled at each other and Melvin said, "Now who said men aren't sensitive and in tune you're your feelings?"

He was still trying to prove a point about the discussion we had on sensitivity. I couldn't analyze the problem right then and there. Melvin had left me feeling the aftershocks of our lovemaking. I loved him so much, I rolled over and the clock caught my eye. It was nine thirty and I looked across the room at the accountant books still on the floor right where we had left them, along with our crumbled heap if clothes. Reality set into my mind and I knew I had to get up right away and start entering the accounts into the new database. Melvin caressed the base of my neck all the way down to the bottom of my spine. I knew I had to get up, so I made the first move. Melvin grabbed my arm and asked me about seconds. I kissed him and gently pulled away, telling him that I had to start on those entries and have them finished by tomorrow.

I went into the bathroom, got into the shower, and let the warm waster cascade over me. It felt so good. I closed my eyes and started thinking of the satisfying feelings that Melvin gave me. I took the sponge and could hardly touch my pocketbook of pleasures. I could still feel pulsations within me from Melvin's touch. I opened my eyes and Melvin was getting in the shower with me, smiling.

"I knew you wanted more," he replied. He still had a lustful look in his eyes and his manhood was still aroused, telling me he wanted more. He grabbed me closer to him as the water fell in between us. He came to my ear and moaned, "I've got to have more of your softness, baby. Your creaminess felt so good around my rod. Baby, I need more of you." His breath heated my insides and I instantly wanted to be taken by him.

To hell with the accountant entries, I thought. He reached down and started rubbing on my swollen pussy mound. I spread my legs and Melvin drove himself deep within my wetness. It was the sweetest satisfaction. He filled every nook and cranny of my hungry tunnel. He plunged into me very slowly. I begged him to go harder; he sustained and granted every wish I had. I was soon to let go of a notorious eruption that had built up in me once again. My walls squeezed him until he could hardly hold on. He started plunging into me faster and faster until I cried out from a notorious cum of satisfaction. We finished taking our shower, dried off each other, and then got dressed for the night.

Sleep was not in my agenda. I went back into the front room and looked at the two accountant books that I had to tackle. It was already getting late and I was starting to feel all the stress that I had got rid of earlier. I turned on my laptop and proceeded to deal with my work. Melvin came in and asked me if I wanted him to make me some coffee or hot tea, and I took him up on the coffee. He prepared it for me and gave me a good night kiss on the cheek. It was only five minutes and Melvin was knocked out, snoring like a baby. My eyes were a little heavy, but I had to concentrate to finish those damn accounts. I started going over the accounts and noticed that it was a much better way to deal with the accounts. I did the work, but I decided that maybe I would tell Susan tomorrow, it would save the company thousands of dollars. My mind drifted once again when I finished the first book.

I started thinking of the way Melvin made love to me. If it weren't for the evening, I don't know if I could get over what Susan had thrown my way. Melvin had smoothed my mind a bit about work. I had never devoted my job beyond the boundaries into my home, it was torture and I felt a violation of my freedom. I did enough for Susan on the job. I started thinking about why she was doing this to me. I'd always kept my distance from her at work, but the more I grew tired the more I started to hate her. Well, I didn't grow with the word hate associated with a person, so I had to scratch that last thought and replace it with dislike her as a person. One thirty am had shown on the clock and my eyes were swollen and filled with sleep. I had finally finished inputting all of the accounts for Susan and my mind was so tired. I started packing up everything and saved all the information, then shut down the computer. Boy, I wished my life was a little different. I thought to myself, *whom is the blame for the way things turned out for me?* I looked up toward heaven and said, "I need a blessing. I know I messed up, but can I get a small break?" I grabbed a piece of paper and had to write something that just came to me.

A Satisfied Black Woman

The road I left behind
Both joys and sorrows it held

With those words, I felt happy that I had thought of them and was ready to turn in for the night.

CHAPTER THIRTEEN

Getting Things In Order

It was seven o' clock and my alarm was going off. I was still tired, but I knew I had to get up and start my day. I looked over and saw that Melvin had gone to work. As the sun rose, its rays touched me as it peeked through my window. I got up, jumped in the shower, and giggled to myself as I thought about last night. I loved him so much I couldn't imagine life without him. But for now, I had to get my head out of the clouds. I got out of the shower, dried off, slipped on my intimates, and reached for my new pant suit that fit just right. I looked on my dresser and grabbed my favorite Vera Wang perfume and lightly sprayed it down my neck and wrist. My hair still held a few curls despite of my heated evening and I brushed it enough to be presentable. I picked up my purse, the accountant books, and was on my way to the door when the phone rang. I looked at my caller ID and it was Sharise. Hell, I had forgotten to get back to my sister yesterday. I knew she was going to give me the third degree about it. I picked up and answered with an apology.

"Sharise, I'm so sorry that I didn't get back with you yesterday. I really got tired up in a lot of drama at work and everything slipped my mind after I wanted to kick my boss' ass." She told me that she understood and I asked her how things were going. Sharise wanted to know if we could possibly go out to lunch and I thought that it would be a great idea. We decided to meet at the Bistro at twelve. I told Sharise I loved her, hung up, and was on my way to work.

As I pulled into the garage, Jerry came out to look at my work pass. "Hey, Shante, you are looking radiant as always this good Friday morning." I was smiling from ear to ear when it came to greeting old Jerry. He was one of those types of people that you would never know if he was having a bad day. His personality was perfect for meeting and greeting. He was also on old confidante of mine. If you needed someone to talk to and listen to you, he was the one. You could tell he had a lot of life experience. He was very intelligent and still was in pretty good shape. He told me to have a great day and opened the gate for me to go in and park. After I slipped in my space, I pulled down the mirror and checked my lipstick and hair to make sure everything was in place. I looked over in the president's space and saw that Susan was already there. I closed my eyes, said a prayer for her and me as well, took a deep breath, and said to myself that I was going to have a good day no matter what. I got out of the car, put the alarm on, and headed for the elevators.

While walking, I started to remember the days I could not wait to get to work. It was such a joy. Life to me now was like opening a birthday gift that you did know what to expect. You put your hand inside, and pull out something that may give you joys or sorrows. My thoughts drifted off again and I started digging in my purse for a pen. When I found one, I pulled out a piece of paper and jotted my thought down quickly before the doors opened.

The road that stands before me
Holds mysteries
Unknown tales

I looked down at my watch and it was eight thirty five. When the elevator opened, I pushed my floor and had a mindset of ready to tackle the world. The elevator seemed to stop on every floor, then finally I was on eight. When I stepped out everyone I passed today seemed to be in a Friday good mood, there were so many chipper attitudes. "Good morning, Shante. Happy Friday." "How are you doing today," was all I heard from just walking down the hall.

I was getting ready to pass Susan's door and saw that it was opened, and before I approached it, I heard Greg talking with her. It was so true on watching your back everywhere you went because as I approached closer without them seeing me, I realized I was in the center of their conversation. I didn't want to call it eavesdropping, but the fact that I heard my name flat out made it sure I was to listen. I heard Greg telling Susan that all I did all day was daydream while looking out the window and doodling writings because one day I thought that I was going to be an aspiring writer or something like that. They both laughed and Susan broke their laughter with, "Well, all I know is that she better have the books recorded and on my desk be nine, or else I hope she gets inspired about that." I knew of Greg's reputation of back stabbing, but Susan was supposed to be a professional. I bit my tongue not to say anything that could be used against me as I walked into her office. I swear I wished Greg was not in there at the moment because I wanted to curse and beat the shit out of her. But, he would have been a witness and I didn't need that, so I quickly dismissed that thought. I walked in and stunned the both of them. I placed the books along with the disk down on her desk.

"Here you are, Susan. Everything is backed up on this disk. Now if you would excuse me, I feel as though I've been inspired to write a few lines before I start my day." Then, I walked out slowly, singing a part of one of my favorite old tunes from the O'Jays. "They smile in your face, all the time they want to take your place, the backstabbers." I left out the jungle with a smile and singing. It felt kind of good that I didn't have to curse her out. But with Greg, I would deal with him in due time.

On my way out, I heard Greg's say, "Oh, no she didn't." That moment, to hear that on my way out was priceless.

I put a smile on my face a mile long. I was not even going to let the two of them ruin my good attitude. That changed as soon as I unlocked my door and noticed another pile of work on my desk. I knew that Susan just couldn't wait to pile it on my desk. She had the balls to unlock my door, come into my office, and lock it back.

Just as my thoughts were jumping to conclusions, Greg came into my office with a stupid grin on his face. "Oh, well I see that you got acquainted with the stack of applications that have to be inputted into the system as well. I left them there for you this morning."

I saw my thinking was a little wrong in thinking that Susan had left the work. "You left them on my desk?"

Greg looked at me and said, "These orders were from your boss, Susan. If you have any problems, take it up with her."

I looked at him and asked him how long had it been since he was demoted to a mail carrier. "Or better yet, I guess you are a wonderful little lap dog for Susan."

Greg's eyes grew furious and he shouted out at me, "Who in the hell are you calling a lap dog, you bitch?"

Our voices were growing louder and started to attract others in the office. I yelled at him and told him he had no right to unlock my door and place anything on my desk. "There is a mail basket right outside my door. If they were so important, you could have waited for me to get to work this morning." Heads were started to peek in my door. I remembered I had to gain my senses and remember what I had promised myself that morning about it being a good day. My phone rang and I saw it was Terrance. Greg looked down at my caller ID to see who was calling. I snatched the phone up and asked him was that all he wanted. He rolled his eyes and left out. I went over to the door, closed it after him, almost letting it hit him where the good Lord split him. I put the phone up to my ear. "What's up, fool? Is everything good?"

"Yeah, it's cool."

"What about you and your new girl, I forgot her name already, did you have a good time the other night?" Terrance started telling me about the nice place he had taken her to and my mind started drifted off to Melvin. I wondered was Melvin thinking of me the way I was thinking of him. I thought the satisfaction of a man's touch stayed with you for a long time. I couldn't stop thinking about it. Every time my mind went there my stomach turned in knots. I guess that was why women were from Venus and men were from Mars.

My thoughts were interrupted. "Shante. Shante, are you still there? Girl, I know you hear me." Terrance was snapping me out of my trance. "Girl, did you hear anything I said to you? Man, Melvin must have laid it on you pretty thick last night because you are still pretty orgasmic from him." We both busted out laughing. Terrance was so crazy. He always knew when something was heavy on my mind. I apologized for not listening very well. I started telling Terrance about last night and he was a little speechless. "Do you want to do lunch later?" he asked.

"I can't today. I promised Sharise I would meet her for lunch." Terrance asked me again about going to The Bistro that night to recite my work and to hear some poetry that we could snap our fingers to when our souls were being touched. I told him that I'd think about it and would call him later.

I pulled up to my desk and tried to start on my work. My eyes were still tired from last night's task. I started yawning and rubbing my eyes, so I got up to go and get a cup of coffee from the main office. I spoke to my co workers as I passed them. I looked ahead of me and as usual, Greg was running his mouth to others who would be listening to his nonsense. When I approached, his conversation ceased and everyone started walking away. I knew that he was talking about me, but I didn't want seem paranoid about it so I just dismissed my feelings and started to pour me a cup of coffee. He started a conversation with me as though nothing ever happened between us.

"Hey, girlfriend, how is it going today?" he asked. He just didn't know what to say sometimes, it had only been about thirty minutes when I just closed the door behind him in my office.

I answered shortly, "Fine," while still stirring my coffee, never looking at him.

He could not take the cold treatment that I was giving him, so he started to try and gossip to get me to talk to him. He tapped me on the arm for some much needed attention. "Look, Susan is getting ready to assign you even more records to input and record. But get this, she told me that you are trying to be so smart with finishing that stuff so quick, so she is going to retrieve more things from the vault for you to record. That stuff is so old, maybe twenty years back, would really be a waste of time on your part to put into this new system, but you keep your records so up to date that's all she could come up with. She is being so vindictive."

It was something about having a female supervisor sometimes that was a struggle. I knew that she couldn't be happy at home. I looked at her life. She was a divorcee, she was alone, even her two kids moved away from her. She had a son and a daughter, and one lived in Utah and the other one, I think, went to New Mexico. That was just sad, wasn't it? She seemed to be married to her job. Susan was coming down towards the coffee machine and Greg tapped my arm and said with such phoniness in his tone.

"Well, girlfriend, I've got to get back to work." He smiled at Susan as he was passing her. "Susan, girl, you are wearing that suit today. You are just looking fierce." Greg really tried too hard. Even women don't carry on that much. He was so flamboyant, and such a great liar. Her suit was ugly as hell, but I was not there to judge, I only observed at times.

Susan came over to where I was standing and started pouring her a cup of coffee. She looked at me and said, "Well, your work was very impressive. There will be more for you to input into the new system," she said.

I looked at her straight in the eye and told her that I didn't appreciate taking all that work home and working on it so late. "I don't mind doing the work in the future here in the office, but I will never take it home with me again because I am off the clock by the time I leave at five."

Susan's eyes grew so wide because she was taken off guard for a moment. She then gained her composure, rolled her eyes, and told me that where she came from, if she had been assigned a job that she would go to any means necessary to finish the job. "This is what it means to have and appreciate, or even keep a job sometimes. I'm sorry I forgot to mention to you about the new contract. We as employees will have to do extra for our reviews to look good for any advancement. This is in effect as of this week."

Oh no she didn't just lecture me on the meaning of having and keeping a job in so many words. It sounded like a little threat. I knew what it meant to have a job. I wanted to point to the clock and tell her that when the clock pointed to five, all I had to show her was my ass leaving out through the door. I wanted to tell her that everything pertaining to the job would stay behind the door after hours, unless there was overtime involved. I wanted to tell her that I had my own life which didn't include Dave and Donavan Associates after hours. I turned and strutted away from her, wishing I had a, 'Yeah, I know I got that bitch straight' attitude. She would have been furious with me if I would have said those things to her. But, there were too many witnesses. I promised myself that there was going to be the place and time for the shit to hit the fan. I bit my tongue and walked away. I didn't know why she had such a power trip going on. I really missed Mr. Harris, but from that moment on, I knew it was going to be on with little Miss Susan and me.

I sat down in my office and started my daily duties. I looked on my list of customers that I had to contact. There were four interested in setting up accounts with us. I had to make nine calls while also recording the existing accounts in the new database. I looked at the first customer, Mrs. Brownstone at 555-1234. I picked up my phone and dialed her. She answered and I went on my daily questions of gaining another client.

CHAPTER FOURTEEN

Sisterly Love

I had made three calls and suddenly glanced at the clock and saw it was time for me to meet Sharise for lunch. I grabbed my compact, put some lipstick on, and grabbed my purse and proceeded out of the building. I walked down to the elevators past Susan's office where I knew the devil was busy because Greg was in her office just like his usual, being a nice little lap dog. God he made me sick.

I was on time when I arrived to meet Sharise. The waiter seated me in a nice spot with a view of the Potomac. He asked me if I wanted to order my drink and I looked down at my watch to see Sharise was ten minutes late. I asked him to bring me a glass of water, and as he was getting ready to walk away, I caught him and told him to make it two glasses of water with a lemon wedge in each. I reached in my handbag and grabbed my phone to call her. Just as I was dialing, Sharise was walking toward the table. I stood up and I gave her a much needed hug. Sharise looked terrible and I could tell that she had been crying for awhile. Her eyes were puffy and swollen.

"I ordered you some water. I was getting worried and was wondering if you had changed your mind. I'm sorry that I didn't get back to you sooner, but I had to deal with a lot of things myself," I told her.

Sharise looked at me and responded to me with a much unexpected comment. "You know you can be a very selfish bitch at times. You sit there with that look on your face like, I feel like you're saying do you really think I have time for this. I called you a few days ago with my life going down the toilet and you put me off. I wanted to talk to you, and you kept telling me in so many words, 'Oh here we go again with this charade of my sister and her boyfriend drama again.' You think that your life is so much better than mine. You think that I am beneath you, don't you, Shante?" Sharise was losing all of her senses it seemed to me.

I went over to her side of the table and hugged her. "I'm sorry, Sharise. I really was dealing with some issues at work. These things could not be ignored. I had to seriously take care of them as soon as possible. I'm sorry." Sharise grabbed a napkin and started sobbing in it. The waiter cane to take our order and I told him to came back in about five minutes. Sharise was finally getting a hold of herself and she apologized for the crying episode. I told her that a good cry was always good for the soul. "Remember Ma used to say everyone needs a good cry now and then to help cleanse the sadness from your soul," I said. We both laughed.

"God knows I miss her," Sharise said.

The waiter came back and we ordered our lunch. I was watching my weight, so I just had the crab salad and Sharise had the same. "So, tell me what is going on?" I asked her.

Sharise told me that she finally had evidence that Vance had been unfaithful to her for the past three months. I asked my sister if she had known or even had this feeling about Vance before. Then, I asked her why she never confronted him when she suspected him instead of knocking herself over and over in her mind with the question of his infidelity. Sharise looked at me and said, "I'm not guessing or wondering about anything here. You know he will never tell the truth. Men will always want their main stuff at home and have his cake outside to eat as well. Vance is fucking around on me," she said, pointing her finger and hitting the table with it.

The waiter had walked to the table at that very moment to serve our salads. His eyes were large with what he had just heard. When he left, I started questioning my sister. "Sharise, what is making you feel so certain that sometime is going on?"

She looked at me and said that Vance had been coming home late for the past two months. "He tells me that he is working overtime, but every time I call his office, he is always on a conference call or in a meeting. He is never around. I feel that his co workers are lying for him. And the phone calls at home, when I answer I get hang ups from the other end."

I put a mouthful of salad in my mouth and chewed slowly, thinking of what I was about to say to her. I had to say it in a delicate manner. I picked up my water, took a sip, and swallowed enough to wash it down. I finally told Sharise what I thought about the situation. "Sharise, every month you have an issue with Vance. When he doesn't come home from work on time you feel that he is out with someone. When you get hang ups on the phone you feel as though there is another female wanting to talk to Vance. You have never heard anybody on the phone, but you just feel that some woman is there on the other end for him. When he doesn't want sex from you, this makes you feel as though he is satisfying some other woman somewhere. And, notice your use of the term sex. It's because that's how you put it all the time in a sentence when it comes to you and Vance. Have the two of you ever made love? I mean, do you know what making love is? It sounds so harsh with the terms you use sometimes. I wish I could let you know how it feels to really be in love with someone like Melvin and I."

Sharise looked at me and said, "I didn't come here for a love lesson from you. You are suppose to be her for me as my sister, someone to listen, give me some advice, and at least have a little sympathy for me. Every time I talk to you about something serious going on in my life, you always seem to want to turn the conversation back around on you." Sharise snatched up her purse and was getting ready to leave.

I grabbed her arm and asked her not to leave. I apologized and tried once again, more interested. I asked Sharise did she have any proof of her accusations. She opened her purse and pulled out a matchbook. I looked at it and it was from the Holiday Inn on Surf Boulevard. "Okay, a book of matches from the hotel. He could have got these from the bar that's in there. "

Sharise told me to open the book and read the cover. There was a message written in ink on the inside. *Call me anytime 555-1508 Clover.* Sharise looked at me and asked, "Well, what do you have to say about that?"

I didn't want to jump to conclusions with her and I didn't want to sound as though I was on his side. I knew deep down that Vance was a dog from the things that he tried with me when I was younger. But, I didn't want to tell her about that now. She would probably not talk to me ever again because I never came to her years ago. How could I have ever done that because she would have never believed me, so I let sleeping dogs lie. Anyway, that's been so long ago. I asked her what she was going to do. "Have you called the number?" I asked.

Sharise told me that she had called and it was a recording of a sex line. "I wanted to talk to her, but I would have to stay on for three minutes until she connected with the line. You know, for the telephone company to connect your number so they can start charging your bill up. I mean, men are so stupid. They never think. I am going to start a little file on him. All the dirt that he does, I am going to get everything on him," Sharise said.

What I don't understand was what she was going to do with the information she had. I had to ask her. "Well, are you going to confront him with anything?"

"As soon as he starts thinking that I am so stupid that I don't know what's going on will be the time I am going to get all in his shit."

"But still, Sharise, what are you going to do?" She never could answer me about her end result what was she going to do. "Are you going to kick his ass to the curb? What?"

She looked at me and told me that's what was driving her crazy. "I just don't know. He has always been the only one for me. He provides for his family very well. I know that he loves me, but I think he has become a little bored with me. Maybe I'm not doing the things that I use to with him sexually. He asked me the other day about how I felt about couples that swap or even a threesome. When he asked me, I looked shocked and he smiled and said, 'No, honey, I only want to know how you feel about stuff like that.'"

I looked at her and told her that I thought that Vance was probably interested in all of that, he was trying to get her feelings on it. "Niggers are always trying to be slick and see what they can get away with. This is a hard, I just don't' know what to tell you. With this one you are going to have to go with your gut feelings and decide about how much you want to put up with and for how long. Think about what's best for you and your children. You know, Sharise, have you ever thought if the shoe was on the other foot. Suppose you would have gone to him with the desire to have him and another guy in the sack at the same time. I would probably be at your funeral right now. The world has such a double standard when it comes to the men of the world. I guess it has been around since the beginning time, cavemen dragging the women out the cave and shit," I told her. I looked around for the waiter. I had to end the conversation and started talking on something else. I looked down at my watch and realized my lunch was just about over. I called for the check and paid the bill, and Sharise and I left out of the restaurant, waved our goodbyes, and I started back to the office.

CHAPTER FIFTEEN

Co- Workers And Drama

I was pulling up in my space and noticed Greg and Susan getting out of her car, I figured they must have gone to lunch together. He never kept a dull moment and I was sure that was an interesting lunch. I wish I could have been a fly on the wall with that one. They both made their way onto the elevator and the doors closed. I did not feel like socializing with either one of them, so I didn't get out of my car until the elevator doors closed. When they both disappeared, I got out of the car, went to the elevators, and pushed for the next ride up. I had four hours left at work, so I went into my office to make the rest of evening productive. Two hours into my work my phone rang. I answered and it was Melvin.

"Hey, baby, what's up?" He sounded so mellow. His voice showered and soothed away all of my bad karma for the day. I just couldn't wait until I was in his loving arms. I was so glad that I had him. I loved him more and more every day. I knew I would be home before him and was eager to please him. I asked him what he wanted for dinner and he told me to surprise him.

"Hey, baby, don't ever tell me that because when you get home, I just may be waiting for you in a big glass dish of whipped cream," I told him. Melvin and I both laughed. He told me that he would be a little late but that he was still was going to want some of my cooking. I told him I would be waiting to serve him. "I love you, Melvin, and I'm going to show you tonight," I told him. He told me the same and we hung up.

I started working some more and Greg passed by looking at me as though he wanted to talk on a friendly basis again. He finally came in on his third time passing and sat down. "Girl, what's up?" He asked.

I didn't respond. As long as he has known me, he knew that I could hold a grudge as long as the cows came home. I never would appreciate the switch he had with Susan. I could imagine the things that he had told Susan about every employee in the office, including me. I probably would forgive him, besides I'd always been the bigger person when it came to forgiveness all my life. He was waiting for me to strike up a conversation with him.

I opened the floor with a sarcastic question. "Well, how was your lunch with your boss lady?"

He looked a little shocked because he probably didn't realize that I knew of his lunch with her. He looked at and said, "Well, you know Susan wanted me to show her a good place to eat lunch at, so I showed her Salads Guru down on third."

"Oh, that's a good place," I told him. I fished around in my purse for my keys. That was the indication of it being the end of my day and that I was not interested in any other conversation with him. I stood up grabbing my coat, and walking back to my desk to log off on my computer. He just looked at me and could not take any more ignoring him, so he tried to strike up my interest with another piece of gossip information.

"Well, you know all the information that you put into the new system? Well, Susan introduced it today in the directives meeting. And you know they loved the way she organized all of that information in. She gave you no credit at all. Ain't that a bitch?" I fell in my desk chair and stared into my computer, thinking of that conniving, brainless piece of shit. I really knew that she was a backstabber. Greg then said, "Honey, if I was you, I would go in her office and kick her fat, white, brainless ass."

"You know, Greg, all I did was organize it, but it is a ton of money that could be saved just reorganizing and revamping the original numbers on each account by using a simple formula like this one." I showed him my calculations of the accounts and he looked intrigued.

"That is impressive. I don't know how they missed that one. You have a good evening." He then walked out. I didn't want to stereotype, but some types of people just had to have drama all up in their areas, Greg was one of those types of people. Even though he was a gossiper, what he had to say always was about ninety percent correct. I felt betrayed by Susan. One mind told me to go and confront her, another mind told me to curse her ass out, and the third mind told me to get her ass back somehow, slowly. I think that I would go with the third; I could be a little vindictive now and then myself. I got up, grabbed my keys, and was off for home.

CHAPTER SIXTEEN

Abrupt Departure

I got in my car, waving, to Jerry as we both told each other to have a good weekend. Jerry released the security arm, allowing me to drive out of the garage and unto the ramp. I was battling back the tears that were trying to form in the corner of my eyes. My face was tightening up from the tension that Susan was overwhelming me with. The sun was just settling with a beautiful orange glow that started to put me in a subtle mood. I needed to get the day's events off of my mind, so I popped in one of my Jill Scott CDs. *I sure could use a good massage tonight. It would be nice if my baby was going to be waiting for me like he did the other day.* I knew that he had spoiled me, and I loved it. I treated him to lots of royalties also. I pulled up to a red light and waited. As an old couple came in the crosswalk in front of my car to cross the street, I thought they were the most adorable elderly couple still in love. My heart just melted. The light turned green and I was startled by a car horn behind me. I must have been daydreaming because I was all wrapped up in the love that showed through them. After the couple crossed, I looked in the mirror at the idiot that had blown me and gave him the 'now is not the time, asshole' look, and proceeded into the beltway, away from the busy city of Washington and into my quiet suburbs of Silver Spring.

I pulled into my driveway and saw that Melvin had got home before me, which puzzled me after he told me that he was going to be late. Oh well, maybe he didn't have to work after all. I started smiling, hoping that he had a surprise waiting for me again. I was hoping that he was going to take me again once I walked through the door. Just the thought had my juices flowing through my panties, which would give him easy admission into my love tunnel again. I got out of the car and went in, and Melvin was in the bedroom. I walked in saw a suitcase on the bed that he was packing. He was looking out of the window and when I walked in the bedroom he turned around and looked at me with a smile. He came over to me, planting a passionate kiss on my lips.

He looked at me and said, "Honey, I know you don't want to hear this, but I have to go to San Diego tonight. I know I should have told you earlier, but I didn't know until ten minutes after we hung up when I got the call from the headquarters. The stores need me for tomorrow's inventory, so we have to start on it tonight." That was the part of his job that I just hated. I felt so disappointed. He looked at me and said, "Let's not start feeling that way again. I thought you were over this type of thing. You know I have to go on call lots of times. This is one those times. I know you will miss me and I'm going to miss you, but it will only be for a week. I will be back with you before you know it. I want you to keep thinking of me so it will be nice and moist for me to get into when I get back."

I could not believe him. He just kept on packing as though it was nothing. I knew that he had to travel, but what I was stunned about was the way he was leaving without any notice. Damn, he didn't even call a sister at work to give me a heads up. I remember when he used to at least call me to meet him at home for a quickie to tie the both of us over until he came back from his business trips. I started thinking about how long he was getting ready to leave a sister high and dry. I was longing for the long, hot strokes he had just given me the night before. My poor pussy would be good and thirsty for another week. What in the hell was going on? Melvin went back to the window looking out, and looked at his watch. Obviously he was looking for a cab or something. I was getting agitated with his behavior.

"What or who are you looking for?" I asked him.

He responded, "What? No one, I was just looking at the tire on my truck. I thought I was getting a flat on the way home." Melvin loved that Toyota Tacoma. He called it Lucy and it was a racy apple red, and his license plate was *hot one*. I knew that it was Melvin's second love, because I better be the first.

He was acing real strange. He finally finished packing and was counting money. He told me that he would leave a hundred dollar bill in his dresser drawer in case I needed some cash around the house. I would usually take him to the airport, and it was strange that he was not saying anything about me driving him. I finally asked him about it and he quickly told me that his company was going to pay for the parking of his truck. Something was definitely not right because he would never leave Lucy in the airport parking lot for a week. That was the first indication that either I was on a reality show or I was in the twilight zone, or something shady was going on with my man. I always took him to the airport, now even that last little bit of us being together was gone, too. What agitated me even more was that he didn't seem to mind one bit. Maybe I was being selfish, damn it, I was going to miss him. A tear was welling in the corner of my eye and I walked out because I was trying to suck it up. He grabbed his suitcase, kissed me one last time, and told me that would call me as soon as he got there. I walked him to the door and kissed again before he left. I closed the door and peeked through the curtain to get a last glimpse of him leaving. As he drove down the street, another blue pickup with dark tinted windows pulled off from a space also. It seemed odd, but I didn't think anything else about it. My mind started to wonder why Melvin didn't check his tire again. He could have checked it better when he left out, and I never saw him bend down to check it. That seemed odd at that point, but maybe I was just thinking too suspiciously, so I let that thought go.

CHAPTER SEVENTEEN

Suspicions Are On The Rise

That night, I went to the freezer and took out a chicken Lean Cuisine frozen dinner, put it in the microwave, set the timer for five minutes, and went into the bedroom to slip into something more comfortable for the evening. My mind could not get off of Melvin's erratic behavior. I undressed and looked at my cocoa slender figure I still had from high school in the dresser mirror. I was always conscious about everything and what I put in my body for nourishment and sometimes I wondered if not having any children had anything to do with me keeping my figure. The beeping from the microwave broke my concentration on the fitness of my body to let me know that my dinner was ready. I put on of Melvin's large shirts on and ran into the kitchen. Just as I was getting my dinner out, the phone rang.

"Oh thank God," I said to myself, thinking that it was Melvin, maybe telling me how much he'd miss me already, but it was Sharise. I was disappointed because I really wanted to hear Melvin's voice. I answered the phone, wondering what it could be this time that she had found. I knew that was not being fair thinking on my sister's behalf, so I tried to sound optimistic when I answered the phone. "Hey, Sharise, are you feeling better?" I heard the sobbing and I wondered what it was I would have to give her a pep talk about. I was not in the mood and needed someone to give me a talking to my damn self. "What's going on now, Sharise?" She tried holding back the sounds of her distress, trying to talk as normal as possible.

"Well, I found out that Vance is seeing another slut. Someone named Alana. As you might know, she is much younger than me. He was so stupid he left another piece of paper lying around with her name and phone number as well on the table between books on his side of the mattress. I couldn't help myself, I called the number and a woman also answered the phone. She kept saying hello and I was speechless, could not say a word back to her. Then, I hung up."

I asked how she felt about that. "You are probably just as thirsty for answers as you were before you called the number."

She said she was puzzled as hell because she started feeling maybe it was no harm in it. "Why would he leave it right where I could find it? Maybe I am overacting and it's nothing."

I told her that maybe Vance was using reverse psychology on her so she would believe the latter explanation. "Think about it. Like we always have said, niggers are always trying to be slick."

Sharise was frustrated and was ready to call the number back and talk to the woman who answered the phone. I quickly advised her against that because she didn't' know what or she was dealing with. Especially not knowing what was going on, I didn't want her get her hurt. I told her to hold tight until something more solid came her way. "You know, Shante, you are so lucky. I'm always wondering is that person fully there, his mind, body, and soul. Does he belong to me, or is he being shared with someone else? The thought is pure agony and it feels as though you have got the short end of the stick in life. It hurts. Just be glad you do not have to feel that." There was a long silence between my sister and I, because little did she know I was beginning to feel a little suspicion in my own backyard.

Sharise was so angry with herself for not using the right judgment for really seeing things for what they really were. I didn't think that Sharise should beat herself up over it anymore. I told her that she was a good woman and since he never kept his word about marrying her, Vance didn't deserve her. So many women devoted their lives to men and when the men got tired of them, they were ready to throw them back for a newer and younger model and it just wasn't fair. Sharise told me that she just had to call the number and find out if anything was going on between them. I knew my sister had been tormented for years with things that she was suspecting. I decided to back her up on this, but I told her that she needed to get a plan figuring out how she was going to handle everything, and that if she was planning to leave Vance, that she would definitely had to have a plan to make it on her own. She told me that she was definitely going to think about it.

"Shante, I know that you're younger than me, but believe it or not, I look up to you. And I'm scared to try and make it on my own. I feel as though I have been in prison for a long time. I can't even imagine doing anything by myself. I just don't think I can make it. If I decide to do this, will you help me?"

"Of course I will." We said goodbyes, and then hung up.

I looked up at the clock and it was twelve thirty. My mind had started to think the worst about Melvin since he hadn't called yet. *Did he make it there? Was he in an accident?* I picked up the phone and dialed. It started ringing and on the fifth ring, I heard his voice and started feeling relieved. "Baby, where are you?" I asked without even just to say hello first.

I didn't hear anything and realized I had gotten his voicemail when I heard the beep. When the tone came on, I left my message disappointingly. "It's Shante," I mumbled in the phone with my heart sinking with disappointment. I told him to please call me as soon as he got in. I hung the receiver up and glanced at one of my doodling pads. I picked up a pen alongside it and started wring my thoughts and feelings.

> *Sometimes good, sometimes bad*
> *Is what I have been told*
> *A satisfied black woman*
> *Will I ever know?*

I must have drifted off to sleep with my head on the table and the pen still in my hand. When I awoke, it was three in the morning. I knew I was going to be dead tired. I looked at the phone on the table and remembered that I hadn't heard from Melvin. I picked it up once again attempted to dial his number. Even though I knew it was late, I needed some piece of mind to know if he arrived alright. I dialed the numbers and to my surprise, Melvin finally answered the phone in a sleepy, groggy voice

"Hello."

I shut my eyes, looking toward the ceiling, thanking God he answered. "Melvin, why didn't you call me to let me know that you were there? I have been worried sick about you," I told him. I could tell that Melvin was sleeping. He cleared his throat and told me that he had got in late and didn't want to wake me at such a late hour. I felt relieved and let him get back to sleep. "Okay I'll call you back tomorrow. Love you." Then, we hung up. I had to drag myself into the bedroom to catch the rest of my sleep without worrying about Melvin. I finally dozed off, hugging Melvin's pillow real tight.

CHAPTER EIGHTEEN

Agitators

The sound of chirping birds and a nudge of sunlight hitting the side of my face woke me up to a beautiful Saturday morning. God, it felt so good not having to go into the office that you absolutely hated. My phone started ringing just as it always did like clockwork on best friend's weekend out, a tradition Angie and I had started a couple of years ago. I picked up. "Hey, girl, what's crackin'? Get up, you know we got to get our toes done so our men's can suck on them if they want to." We both burst out in laughter.

"Girl," I said, "you are so damn ghetto fabulous." I told her that it didn't even matter about my toes because Melvin was gone on a trip. Angie and I decided to still go and spend the day together.

We started the day at the nail salon. My tension seemed to just melt away while sitting in the massage chair there. The warm water felt so soothing. It would be another ten minutes before my attendant would come back to finish my foot massage and paint my toes. I chose the sea water blue, thinking the color would go perfect with a new dress I had just bought from the Charrie's Boutique. I closed my eyes and was in complete solitude. Angie sat to my right and was enjoying the same rewards as I was. My relaxation was broken by a ghetto acting chick that came in with her friend. When I opened my eyes, they sat across from us popping their gum and letting everybody in on their conversation. I leaned my head back, trying not to look at them, but it was obvious they didn't care. The tall one had really loud colored blond hair cut in a symmetric style which fell down her face in the front like a peacock. She did most of the talking.

"Well, I ain't playing with his ass tonight. He better recognize that he don't just have babies with that holier than thou bitch only. He gots to take care of mine, too. He has been trying to keep this secret about the two of us so long from his wife. Girl, I have not gone downtown on him, but I will in a minute if he ain't taking care of things the way he should, and I mean everything. Child, that pole of his got me hooked like a fish being caught up in deep sea water." The two of them burst out in laughter. The other girl who she was talking to stopped laughing when she looked over at us, like she was disgusted about the way we were looking at them. The tall one didn't care one minute about what anybody thought of her. She continued on saying that if he only had missed a beat on anything, money, spending time with their kids, or satisfying her, she would go downtown on him and file for child support on him in a minute.

Her friend looked at her. "Damn, girl, you are running him ragged and out of his mind. How long do you think he can keep this up? It's a wonder he can even get himself up for your ghetto ass coochie."

"I don't care, as long as he keeps it satisfied. But the minute he slacks up, it's down to the courthouse I go. I know he is sweating bullets every minute when thinks about it. But hey, it makes him fuck me even harder. You know next weekend I told him I want two nights with him so he is going to tell his wife that he has to attend the men's retreat. Girl, he booked us in a nice place."

"Man, he gots to be nervous knowing that you all are in the same church congregation." They both busted out with laughter. "Hallaluur."

My mind started thinking on Melvin and his strange behavior. The nail attendants finished with our feet, and we paid them and left out the door. It wasn't a minute too soon enough for me, I hated being around ignorant people. My mind was wondering why was she in the church, but my mama always did say that the devil goes to church, too. She was the prime example of that.

We started walking down the street on our way to Giovanni's around the corner, it was my second favorite place to eat. When we arrived it wasn't crowded yet, so we were immediately seated. He gave us a nice table in the back, then gave us menus and told us about the special for the day. I ordered a shrimp salad and Angie had the shrimp scampi. We ordered two glasses of white wine, and then we started our conversation about that chick in the nail salon. We laughed and talked about the good old days. Before we knew it an hour had gone by. We left feeling good and full. Angie had to go to prepare herself for a showing, so we hugged and waved goodbye as we went to our cars. I wondered what I would do for the rest of the evening.

When I got into the car I looked down at my phone for any messages from Melvin and there were none. It was just strange and my mind was being fueled even more from that chick I had just heard. It really made me wonder. I started my car and headed home when my cell rung. Before I pulled off, I answered it hoping that it was Melvin, but it was Terrance.

"What up, Shante?"

"Not a thing. I'm just getting ready to leave the mall and go home. Angie and I was just hanging out today around the mall."

"Well, how is everything on the home front?" I told Terrance that it was sort of the same. "Why don't you come over if you are bored," Terrance asked.

"Well, I guess I could stop by for a little bit. Okay, I'm on my way."

CHAPTER NINETEEN

Everything Has Its Season

I pulled up to Terrance's place and he was standing in the door acting as though he was looking around for backup, he was so crazy. I was smiling as I walked in. "Hurry up, girl. We don't want anybody to see you."

"Shut up, Terrance." He closed the door behind me. I sat down on my usual spot, picked up the remote, and turned on the flat screen.

Terrance came in the room clearing his throat. "Umm, excuse me, but are you home? Is this our place? Did you ask permission?"

As usual, I gave him the same line. "Shut up, Terrance. Where are my refreshments?"

"Why did call you over to get abused in my own place damn?" We laughed and talked for a good hour. He was the picker upper. Then, all of a sudden tears just started falling from my eyes. It took him by surprise. "What's wrong, Shante?"

I couldn't even begin to tell him how I felt. "I just can't put my finger on it. Something is not right in my life." Terrance began wiping my tears, and then he embraced me. He looked at me then pulled me to him. It took me by surprise.

"What just happened here?" I asked.

"I hate to see you hurt, Shante. I got a confession to make. I've always loved you, but being the way things are, I know it's not right. It takes a hell of a lot of restraint not to want you, but I do. I wish I could make you happy. Every time I see you hurt, believe me, I hurt too." We sat down on the couch and Terrance laid me down and got on top of me. "Umm, Shante, I've wanted you for so long. I love you, girl."

My eyes had closed and I was getting swept up by all of it. It was feeling so good until I let my mental state come back into focus. What the hell was I doing? "No, stop, Terrance, this is not right."

He got off of me and started apologizing. "Damn, I'm sorry, Shante. Man, I'm so sorry."

"It's okay, Terrance, you're not to blame. We both were allowing it to happen. We just got caught up.

He got up and looked out the window. "I always promised myself that I would never do that, but I do love you. We have so much history together. But, I shouldn't have allowed myself to do that when I know that you are vulnerable right now. Forgive me, please." He was really beating himself up over this.

I walked over to him and kissed him on his cheek. "Don't worry about it okay, Terrance. You have never wanted me to hurt over things like this. I feel the same for you." Then, I jokingly told him that I thought he was lying and started laughing. "What about all those girls you would bring around to meet me?"

"Hey, I had to do something. I couldn't have you." We both started laughing again. I told him that I better get home and Terrance walked me to the door.

I gave him another kiss on his cheek. "Stay sweet." We smiled at each other then I left for home.

As I was walking up to my door, I heard the telephone ringing from the inside. I hastily found the key, inserted it, dropped everything once inside, and ran picked up the phone. "Hello."

There was a silence and a half of a, "Hello," as though I caught someone by surprise. Then, there was a click followed by a dial tone. I figured they had the wrong number. I looked at the caller ID but it was unknown number. I went back and closed the door, then looked toward the bedroom and started to wonder. My mind was starting to think about was I being played all this time. I looked at his dresser drawer and all of a sudden I felt a little curious about Melvin's strange actions when he left. When I thought about it, I knew I was just being silly and paranoid. I guess that woman in the salon had my mind wondering. I had an empty nest to come home to, and it made me wonder what if Melvin had kids with another woman elsewhere and gave an excuse of working away when he went to visit them. Ma always used to tell Sharise and I that men would always try and be slick. You would always have to watch them, and never let your guard down.

I sat down on the couch listening to nothing but silence. I hooked my I pod up and started listening to some music. Got To Give It

Up was rocking by Marvin Gaye. I stood in front of the mirror rocking my hips and swaying my butt to the beat. I swayed into the kitchen for something to drink while wiping off the counter at the same time as I passed it. After Marvin's tune started fading away, the next selection came on. It was Teddy Pendergrass telling me to come on and go with him. I went into my purse and pulled out all of the pieces of paper I had written all off the parts of my poem on. I took a clean sheet and wrote everything that I felt and was pleased.

A satisfied black woman
Will I ever know?
A lifetime of thinking and wondering
Which way I really should go
The road I left behind
Both joys and sorrows it held
The road that stands before me
Holds mysteries
Unknown tales
Sometimes good, sometimes bad
Is what I have been told
A satisfied black woman
Will I ever know?

I felt excited and liberated after I felt the words on paper representing my soul. I wanted everyone to hear.

CHAPTER TWENTY

Something Just Ain't Right

The day had come when Melvin was due back from his trip. I missed him terribly and I couldn't wait for his arrival. It had been odd for me with him not calling every night like he used to do. It had my mind playing tricks on me. Every other influence aside from that was definitely feeding into it. I meditated for an hour, thinking on a perfect setting for my baby when he arrived. My meditation made me feel like a new woman, mind, body, and spirit. I got up and started preparing a romantic dinner for us. The lobsters were in the freezer with rubber bands around their claws, and I waited to give them their final spa treatment. I looked at the clock, trying to time myself perfectly with him walking through the door. I placed two russet potatoes in the stove, looked at the clock, and realized I had one hour. I jumped into the shower and smiled as the water splashed into my face. After my shower, I primped in the mirror and thought that I would only come to the door with my apron on. I would like him to eat dessert before dinner. I went into the kitchen and checked the potatoes, which were ready. I heard keys in the door and Melvin was walking through. Damn, he was early, but a real sight for sore eyes. I didn't have time to put the lobsters in the pot. He looked and me and smiled. I grabbed him and we gave each other a much needed embrace.

"Oh, you're cooking?"

"I hope you're hungry for lobster and me," I told him. Just the mere sight of him made my mouth water.

Melvin's smile started looking a little sour. "Babe, I'm sorry, something I ate must have upset my stomach from the plane and my head is killing me."

I was disappointed, but my baby was sick. I walked him to the bedroom, helped him get into the bed, and gave him a kiss. "I love you."

He told me the same.

I went to the dresser and pulled out a large shirt and underwear and put them on. I was disappointed as hell, but I had to be considerate. My baby wasn't feeling well, and that was that. I grabbed the cordless phone and took it out so he wouldn't be disturbed. I went in the kitchen and started boiling the water for the lobster. When it was ready, I placed the head first, and then steamed them to perfection. I fixed a plate, and tipped quietly to check on Melvin. He may have been feeling a little better and may wanted a little of the food once he get a whiff of the smell. I tipped quietly up to the door and the closer I got, I heard Melvin talking to someone, but to whom? I knew I had taken the phone out. As I got closer I heard him telling someone, "That it was alright, but next time I hope that it won't last so long." When I opened the door, Melvin had moved on his side and turned around in the bed.

"Melvin, were you just talking to someone?" He looked up at me as though I had awakened him.

"No," he answered in a sleepy voice.

"Oh, I'm sorry for waking you up."

"It's okay, babe," he said in a sleepy, groggy tone. I asked him did he want something to eat and he told me he didn't, but he asked me to bring some ginger ale to help settle his stomach. I kissed him again and told him I would.

I closed the door feeling very puzzled. I knew I heard him talking to someone. I looked in Melvin's jacket for his cell phone and I couldn't find it. He had to be on the phone, but why was he lying to me? I finally came to the realization that maybe he was so tired that he was snoring. Sometimes when people were so tired that they snored so loud and it could sound as though they were talking, so I dismissed any negative thoughts and went to get his ginger ale.

Morning had arrived and it was time to start another week. The birds were chirping as always to tell me that it was time to get up, and I almost forgot my baby being home. I smiled at the thought and reached over for him, but I only felt an empty space. I got up calling for him. "Melvin."

I heard him stirring around in the front room. He was on the phone and hung up as soon as he heard me. Melvin turned around smiling, greeted me with a hug, and kissed me on my cheek. I asked him who he was talking to and he told me he had to call in to see if he had to make a delivery, and if so where to. My hopes were building on him not having to go in because I was going to be right there with him for the day, but I was disappointed because he said that he did have to make a few deliveries. Melvin told me that he was feeling one hundred percent better, and he thought that he'd better go and make the rounds and go to the office to check on inventory since he had not been there for a week. I felt disappointed, but I understood that it was part of his business. I pouted with my agreement, and then went off into the bathroom to get ready for work. Melvin knocked on the door and casually told me that the contract with my company had been dropped from his regional office.

"What are you saying?" I opened the door and was upset that I wouldn't see him at the office anymore. Melvin wasn't nearly as upset as I was. "I mean when did this happen? Why didn't you tell me this?" I would miss him coming into my office. His deliveries were a bit of spice that we had put in our marriage. Even though we were married, I pretended at that moment that I was being a bad girl at work, like it was so many years ago when we first met. All Melvin did was look at me with a frown and told me that it was not that serious.

"Calm down, baby, I'll give you the same goodies at home, too." He kissed my forehead and I finished getting ready for work.

Work was easy going until noon, that's when Greg came in trying to pluck my nerves. I was determined that not even Greg would get next to me, I would to kill him with kindness. I knew that after work was over my evening was going to be a hot. I had been waiting for a week for my pulsating pussy to meet up with its master. Greg came in my office and sat down.

"Hey there, Shante, girl, what do you know good?" He was acting as though nothing had happened last week between us at work. I was going to be the bigger person and forget all about that petty stuff. Greg started talking about Susan and all of her personal business that he knew about. If only she knew that she was dealing with a two sided coin. I turned and started my usual gazing, looking outside the window as he talked. Everything that was coming from his mouth was sounding like an old Charlie Brown cartoon when the teacher was talking to Charlie's class. "And you know that Katrina down the hall was caught, blah, blah, blah, blah, blah, blah." I continued to let him talk, but didn't understand a word that was coming out of his mouth, reason being, I wasn't interested in what he was talking about. I just wanted him to get the hell out. Greg noticed my uninterested stare and I think he took it in offense, so he got up and left.

My mind was still on Melvin losing his contract with the company. Every two weeks I had something to look forward to, now all I could do was have anticipation on my thoughts of what used to be. I was wondering did Susan have anything to do with him losing the contract. I guess I should have talked to Greg because he may have had some information on it. Oh well, if he had any knowledge of it, he would spill the beans soon. I got a grip on myself, looked at my desk of duties, and started conquering my work for the day. Just as I was almost finishing my tasks for the day, my phone rang. On the other end was a mysterious woman's voice.

"Look, Mrs. Brenin, you don't really know me, but I'm just calling you to let you know that the man you married is really not who he appears to be. He has a lot of skeletons in his closet."

"Who is this?"

"Look, all I'm saying is being careful and watch him more closely."

"Hello, who is this?" I got a hang up after that. When I looked at the number I redialed and called back. It rang and it was a lot of noise in the background.

"Hello. Hello." Someone picked up the phone and I asked the person did they just call this number. "No, miss, this is a pay phone booth. " I asked where was it located they told me it was in New York. I hung up and was wondering who would be calling me from New York. It stayed on my mind until it was almost time for me to leave for home. I dismissed it as somebody messing with me and I came to the conclusion that it was some sick, jealous person.

I looked up at the clock and was glad that it was five o'clock, time to end the day. I packed up my belongings and headed for the elevators. I got in my car, waved goodbye to Jerry, and headed for home along with thoughts of excitement as I wondered about what Melvin may have waiting for me. It had been so long since Melvin and I had been connected. Okay, technically it had only been a little over a week, but I had the hots for the man. Even though I had my suspicions about him, sometimes one thing in my mind would outweigh the other. My body was aching and I needed him.

As I pulled up in the driveway, there was a car besides Melvin's parked in my driveway. To my surprise, it was Melvin's brother, David. I'd only seen David a couple of times and the last time was at our wedding; he was in the wedding party, a replacement at the last minute for the best man. Melvin's best friend had an emergency and had to leave, and although David was a groomsman, he volunteered and stepped in to stand by his brother. I thought it meant a lot to Melvin at the time. David seemed generally happy, which made me even happier. When Melvin and I kissed at the wedding and turned around to be presented as Mr. and Mrs. Melvin Brenin, I caught David wiping a tear from his eye. I felt from that moment on, that whatever bitterness they may have had in between them was probably melting away. My hopes seemed to be true, because we began to see more of David. I was happy to see Melvin and his brother become closer, but this was the one day that I wished he wouldn't have made a visit because I was ready to get my freak on with my man.

Once inside, sitting on the couch was David and some young, cute girl, and Melvin. They were in the living room looking at some porn flick. "What the hell?" Melvin reached for the remote and clicked it off. The girl turned with a smile.

She snickered and said, "Busttted."

David turned around and said, "Well, if it ain't the sexiest sister in law around." He came over to me and hugged me.

I mumbled, "Okay, what are you all up to in my house?"

Melvin came over. "Baby, we were just looking at some tripped out movie that people at my job were talking about."

I asked him what was so fascinating about it and they were all talking at the same time. I really didn't understand either of them, so finally the girl introduced herself to me. "Hi I'm Lucinda Brown. I've heard so much about you, only good things." She shook my hand with a smile and I told her that she should excuse my husband and brother in law's manners. She had on green shorts with a tube top with a black short jacket over it, and for good reason because if she made the wrong move in it her big double Ds would have popped out and been all over the place. She wore the highest spiked heels that I had seen in a long time.

David stepped in saying, "This is my love that I wanted you all to meet." He grabbed her hand, pulled her down next to him, and planted a kiss on her lips.

"Okay, guys, get a room," I jokingly said. We all started laughing.

David stood up. "Okay, which one?" He pointed to our bedroom.

Melvin stood up and said, "Hey, no vacancy at this inn. Don't even try that. Besides, that room is reserved for something good. It has been a long time coming." We all laughed.

I went to the kitchen and asked anyone if they wanted a drink. Lucinda asked for wine and David asked for a beer. Melvin came in to help me with the drinks, pulled out a bottle of Sutter Home Moscato from the wine cooler, and started opening the bottle as I pulled glasses from the cabinet. He brought the bottle over and started pouring. When he finished pouring, he came up behind me and started kissing me in the back of my neck. Melvin ordered Chinese food, then put some music on and pulled out the cards.

"Anybody for a game of spades?"

"Yeah you're on," David said while running over to the table.

When the food arrived we all sat around the table while I pulled out and served the shrimp egg foo young, shrimp fried rice, and served an egg roll on all four of the paper plates. We had good conversation while we listened to old jams that we all listened to in high school. I guess that didn't apply to little Miss Lucinda but she enjoyed it anyway. After we ate, we started our game of spades and played for hours with Melvin and I winning the last round. Lucinda slammed her hand of cards down and stood up walking over to her purse.

"Hey, guys, I got something here you all will enjoy. I picked it up last night at the video store and haven't watched it yet." Lucinda went inside of her purse and took out a DVD. It was called *Just What the Doctor Ordered*. David went over and his eyes got big as he looked over the cover of the movie.

"Oh, this is what I'm talking about, let's get this show started. Hey, can we have some drinks, sister in law, dear?"

"Okay, coming right up." I got up and went toward the kitchen for some beers. David was setting up the DVD player for the movie.

Melvin came in the kitchen and started kissing me behind my ear. "Baby, I just want you to promise that you'll have an open mind about the movie that we are getting ready to see."

"What about the movie? Is it a boring movie or a bad movie?"

"Look, Shante, it's a triple X rated movie okay, so just give it a try."

"What do you mean? Why does she want to see something like that around us? I mean, isn't that sort of a thing for couples to watch alone? This is just awkward for me, Melvin."

Melvin turned me around toward him and pulled me up to him. "Look, baby, lose the ice for me tonight, okay? Just try this one time, you might like it." He kissed me and I reluctantly said yes.

The movie had come on, and I handed everybody their beers. Melvin turned the lights out and the first image was a girl lying on her deck, waiting for a guy that was staring at her and not too soon after the look, they immediately starting engaging in rough house sex. David got close to Lucinda. I looked up at Melvin and he was fixated on the screen, it seemed like almost mesmerized in what the couple in the movie was doing. When I glanced over again at David and Lucinda, they were intimately kissing and touching as though was getting ready to get their freak on right then and there. I felt they were being totally inappropriate. After another actor came in to join them, I just couldn't take it any longer. I got up and cut the lights on, and went up to the DVD and turned it off. I startled them.

"Hey, baby, why did you do that? We were trying to watch the movie."

"I think it's time for us to get to bed, it's getting late."

"Okay, let's go, baby, and watch the rest of this at your house." Lucida and David took the DVD out and left.

Melvin locked the door and turned around with a disgusted look. "Why in the hell did you embarrass me like that? All we were doing was looking at a movie that-"

I didn't let him finish when I jumped in. "All you were doing was getting hot and horny, watching a fuck movie with other people in the room. I mean God, Melvin, it looked to me like to me that David and Lucinda were getting ready to go for it right here on our floor and you probably would have been okay with that."

"You know what, Shante, you are making so much of this silly little incident. You need to stop being so uptight. What do you say that we just forget about this and go and make up in the bedroom?"

"I know you must have bumped your head. Let me tell you how I am thinking at this minute. Your ass is probably still thinking about that nasty little whore on that movie. You still thinking about her, aren't you? Well who will you be thinking about when we get in the bedroom? You touching all over me, will you be really thinking about me or that little slut on the movie? Is she turning you on or will it be me? You know, Melvin, I'm not thinking about any of that tonight. I just want to go to bed and go to sleep because I have to get up for work in the morning."

I went in the bedroom, changed, and got in the bed. Melvin was right behind me and turned the light out. It was only a few minutes after all of that when Melvin got in the back of me and started spooning me, letting me know that he had a hard on. I couldn't believe him. I would not move.

"Baby, come on now, you know I don't believe in going to sleep angry. What do you say if I apologized right now? I'm sorry, I don't know what I was thinking about tonight."

"You know, Melvin, I really think that you are not saying that from your heart, I think you're saying it from your stiff ass dick that is ready to get up in me, but I am still angry because I didn't appreciate your behavior tonight. I feel that you are thinking of the slut you seen on the movie not me, so I want you to think about that." I turned around, and turned to him again and said, "You can't have this tonight, too bad that bitch on the movie can't come out of the screen for you because I feel that's who you are thinking about. I'm not putting out for you tonight, just go to sleep."

Melvin grunted, "You know what, Shante, sometimes you can be a real bitch."

"Whatever." I turned around and tried my best to get some sleep.

CHAPTER TWENTY ONE

Backstabbing In The Office

The telephone rang, startling me and waking me up. I reached over, knocking down several items that were on my night stand. I could not open my eyes because they were so heavy. I finally felt the receiver and answered with a slurred speech. "Helllllllllllo."

"Shante, girl, where are you? You are an hour and a half late. We are having a meeting in thirty minutes."

I hung up the phone and immediately sat straight up in the bed much too quickly because I felt as though there were ten miniature people taking turns slapping me from every angle on my head. My head was banging. Melvin had already left and I was thinking why didn't he wake me? I started contemplated in my head of calling in, but my good senses told me that it wasn't a good day for that, besides I just remembered I had to give a presentation. My pounding head would not let me forget the night that I should have put off until the weekend. I took a ten minute shower, got dressed, pulled my hair back in a ponytail, and then finally left out the door without my morning coffee. I jumped in my car looking at the time. I had ten minutes to get downtown to make it for the meeting. It was obvious that I was going to be another twenty minutes late. I was going so fast until I ran a red light and hoped the camera didn't catch me. Luckily, there were no cars coming across in the intersection, it that would have been a real disaster. I had to get it together, so I pulled over and as much as I hated to, I dialed Susan's extension.

"Hello, Dave and Donavon, Susan speaking."

"Hi, Susan, I'm sorry, but I'm going to be about another twenty minutes late. I wasn't feeling well last night, so I took some medicine that made me sleep so hard that I didn't hear my alarm clock going off. I'll be there soon."

Susan gave out a loud sigh. She finally said, "Don't forget about your presentation," then she hung up. She was such a rude bitch. I looked in my left side view mirror and pulled off.

When I pulled up to the booth Officer Jerry was not there and I figured he was off. It was another guard named Walter who seemed very flirtatious. "Well, hello there, Ms. Brenin. How are you today?" He was coming out off the booth as though he was going to start a conversation. I really didn't have time for it, so I held my left hand up as though I was one of the Supremes.

"Stop, I don't have time for talking. I'm already late, would you please just release the security arm and let me through. And by the way, it's Mrs. Brenin, not Ms. Brenin."

He looked at me and said under his breath, "You little stuck up bitch."

I went through when the arm went up. When I was through, I put on brakes, looked back through my window, and said, "I heard that."

I looked in the mirror and ran my hands through both sides of my hair. I did the best that I could with it, and then darted for the elevator. When I reached my floor, I went into my office, grabbed my presentation, and went into the conference office, and there were fourteen colleagues sitting around the oval table waiting for me. I sat beside Susan, apologized for my lateness, and then began my presentation.

"Based on the numbers and the way we keep our records, this is where it leaves our company today. Are there any questions?" Nobody asked any questions, so I sat down.

Greg stood up with a portfolio and asked everyone if they would mind sitting through a short revised presentation that he thought would save more money than the one I had just presented. I sat down, and then Greg began. He explained to everyone that my numbers were based on something that we did years ago. Then, he showed more up to date numbers and he presented the formula that I showed him in my office not long ago to save money on these accounts. I was in a complete time zone and was shocked. I saw him talking, but I was stunned. Right after I told him about that, he must have gone straight into her office and was getting the credit for something that should have been mine. I knew it, but Susan had me spend my time on those books which were all very old and not up with today's numbers. Greg had to have been working on that the same time Susan gave me the books that were not even being used anymore. Of course, he got the praise and support that everyone wanted to work with the updated system. It seemed like a conspiracy, a well thought out plan just to make me look a fool in front of everyone.

The meeting was adjourned and I started gathering my things. Greg came over to me. "Shante, girl, that was a great presentation. But, this new way of doing things came to me about a week ago. I have been meaning to bring it to your attention, but you are one hard person to get in touch with. Oh yeah, I would have ran it past you this morning, but that's right, you were late, so I'm sorry about this being all new to you like this."

I looked at him. "I can't believe you." He had such a smirk look when he smiled. "I can't believe you," Before I could finish with him, Susan who was still sitting down at the head of the table spoke up.

"Shante, would you please have a seat." I sat down and waited to hear what she had to say. When Greg left out she began talking. "You know, Shante, you have been here at this company longer than I have, but there comes a time when things that you have grown used to have to change as well. This is that time for you right now. Things are going to change. I will be putting Greg in charge of the new system to implement it and get it started. If he needs any assistance, you will be the one helping him. I thought that by giving you this assignment you would have made changes to make it more efficiently, but I see now that you are not a person that makes changes happen, you just stick with routines." She was cutting into me really deep with her words.

"I only did what you asked for. You told me to input the records, you never said change anything."

Susan stood there just shaking her head from side to side saying, "No, no, no," as though I was a child. "I don't want to suspend you or even fire you, but I want this company to grow. There is not enough room for mistakes or slow progress. I can't put anything in your personnel folder such as high praises or any good remarks on this project. This fiasco is going to force me to demote your yearly salary pay down two thousand a year until you can go by Greg's example of making positive changes. You will be promoted if I see changes that you are making to prove for the good of this company." I was convinced that

that bitch was crazy and definitely bipolar.

As I walked back to my office in a daze, I heard Greg telling the other workers about his promotion and a thirteen hundred dollar bonus. That witch had it all planned. They were setting me up. I knew Greg thought it up and they both plotted, having me do all of that useless inputting of those old ass records, it all was just a waste of my time. I guess that was to get me off of what was really going on. I should have never showed Greg the new way of doing those numbers. He just ran with it. They really showed my ass up at that presentation, and to add insult to injury, she demoted me.

Once inside my office, I put my things down and dashed off for the ladies room into a stall where I needed to let out a good cry. The more I cried the more my head pounded. I reached into my pocket and pulled out two Excedrins that I had wrapped in a tissue and placed in my pocket earlier that morning. I listened out for anyone in the bathroom and didn't hear anything. I dashed over to the sink, caught some running water in my hand, and swallowed the pills. With a quick dash, I was back into the stall just before someone came in the restroom. I tried to be a soldier and hold back my crocodile tears. I sniffled until I heard the toilet flush and the sink running water as they washed their hands. The door slammed closed and my tears once again flowed.

After my well deserved cry, I was back in the office trying to get through my work. At the same time, I was trying to figure out what I was going to do next. I thought of my financial situation. It was going to cut some of my independent way of living. Even though I had Melvin and he would do anything for me, I never wanted to burden him with the bills I had before we were married, like my car note or those spur of the moments shopping sprees that I had just on me. It would cut into my savings and everything. My eyes stared to fill up again, but I batted them so they would not well up. I knew I had to call Melvin, so I picked up the phone. I dialed his cell and got no answer. I thought that maybe he went back home already. I started thinking of how Melvin would probably make all my troubles melt away as soon as I get home from work. I started dialing the home phone and it rang three times. Just as I was about to hang the receiver up, I heard the phone pickup and abruptly slam down.

"Hello, Hello?" I tried to connect with Melvin as he picked up. I turned and looked at the receiver. That was strange. I immediately called back and there was no answer. Maybe I dialed the wrong number, so I tried again, and still no answer. I figured I would try again later, so I turned around and started trying to do some work.

CHAPTER TWENTY TWO

Time For Laughter

Around one o' clock my phone rang and it was Terrance. He didn't play any pranks on me, he knew by the sound of my voice that I wasn't in the mood. "Shante, is everything alright? Don't sugarcoat anything, tell me the truth." He analyzed me just from the sound of my voice. I started telling him of the events from last night to this morning. He felt my pain and agreed with me on all that I was feeling, and then he asked about lunch. "Hey, let's go to the waterfront, pick up some lunch, and go to Hanes Point and talk out these feelings. You know I'm your best friend and your damn doctor, too. One day I'm going to send my bill." Terrance laughed. "You need to come and lie on my couch and tell Dr. Terrance about it." He made me smile a little. What the hell, I did need to get out of there. "I tell you what, you just go find a spot and I'll bring the food. Hey, why don't you take off the rest of the day and chill?" That sounded like a good idea, so I told Susan I wasn't feeling well and went to the park to find a spot.

The water swayed beautifully with a nice breeze coming in through the car windows. I lay back in my seat listening to an oldie station. *Be My Girl* was playing by the Dramatics. I closed my eyes, remembering how it used to be when I was younger and my mom and dad were still here. There were no worries, I was just growing up happy. My thoughts were startled by Terrace tapping on my window.

He smiled. "Damn, did I interrupt anything? I mean, I'll wait." I unlocked the door. He always was trying to make me laugh when things are looking down and I was feeling low. "I mean, it don't matter to me. Do you want it in or out?" We both started cracking up.

I looked over and saw a nice bench. "We can go over there at that bench and eat." Terrance handed me the diet Coke and his drink. He ordered two large crab cakes, no fries for me because he knew that I watched what I ate. We sat down and started talking. I thought about Melvin and I told Terrance to excuse me while I tried to call him again.

"Oh, here we go again, dissing me for..." He started snickering as I held my finger up for him to shut up. I dialed Melvin's cell phone while Terrance was making funny faces trying to get me to laugh. I stood up and turned my back. It rang three times and on the fourth ring, he picked up with an exhausting.

"Yeahhhhhhhhhhhh," as though whoever was calling was getting on his nerves.

"Hey, baby, where have you been? I've been trying to reach you all day. Are you alright?" He caught his breath and told me that he was coming out of the shower and didn't want to miss my call again. "Okay, I really need to talk to you earlier. I've had the worst day imaginable. First that bi..."

He cut me off. "Hey, babe, I'm sorry but I've got a plane to catch in two hours for another last minute job in San Diego. I'll only have to stay for a week. I promise we will have more time after I get back. I'm thinking about us going away so think about where you would like to go because we definitely need to catch up with us. I'll miss you, call you as soon as I get there. Love you."

"I love you, too." Melvin had hung up before I could get the last three words out. I couldn't believe how many disappointments I had in just one day. I turned around and walked back to the table. Terrance saw a tear forming in the corner of my eye so he came over to me and gave me a much needed hug.

"What's wrong? Is everything okay?"

Terrance always showed so much concern as I did with him. I kept my head in his chest. I couldn't explain my actions, but I felt a genuine caring feeling at that moment. I tore myself away, then apologized for my over bearing hug. I didn't want to give him any wrong ideas, but at the moment it felt good. We sat back on the bench at our table. I managed to open my crab cake and started eating. I took a sip of my diet Coke and told Terrace what was on my mind.

"Terrance, it seems that Melvin and I are not on the same page anymore. He works so many more hours away from home, out of town. Sometimes it's a week, or a few days, but it's driving me crazy. We don't spend that time with each other like we used to. I miss him, Terrance. I miss his touch and everything."

Terrance looked at me with an, 'I wonder do I have the words for this situation' look. "Come on now, I think your problem is…"

I stopped him before he started and blurted out, "Terrance, I mean, we haven't made love in awhile. It just makes me feel not wanted. I don't feel sexy. I feel that he is not interested in me anymore."

Terrance stopped me from saying anymore. "Now look, Shante, don't start putting yourself down. You know that is not the case. It is nothing wrong with you. You are still sexy and voluptuous as the first day that I met you many years ago. Now I know that Melvin loves you. That man works so much to provide for the two of you. He bends over backwards for you. Shante, it seems that his job is getting to you now. When you married him you knew about his job and what it required him to do. He could be tired, Shante. You know that sometimes plays a part of rough patches between couples. That vacation he wants you to look into sounds like he needs a rest. It will be good for the two of you. Before you know it, your ass will be skipping hop scotch again. And as far as your job, I wouldn't worry too much about that. You know that your man makes enough to take care of everything." Terrance had a gift that God gave him. It was to be a true friend who could comfort and make you feel good about whatever you were feeling so bad about.

We finished our lunch and started walking around the Potomac to alleviate our bellies of that full lunch. People were out strolling, jogging, and fishing. It was such a relaxing feeling in the air. I felt more at eased, even though we were playing hooky from work. Terrace started telling me about his newest love. "Her name is Kenyetta. She is twenty one." I told him that she was barely legal and he continued telling me all about her. He looked at me with a smirk, "Come on now, don't tell me that you're playing the jealous one. Her skin is soft, her breast are perky. Her,"

I looked at him before he could get another word in. "Shut the hell up, Terrance. Are you trying to be funny?"

"What? Why, are you getting jealous?" He was acting as though he didn't know what I was getting at. We laughed and laughed, and continued walking until we felt comfortable will our fullness. We finally got back to the cars and I opened the door and got in.

"Hey, you know we have been friends a long time." I chuckled. "We have something like a best friend history. Nobody would ever understand it, but we both know what it's all about. We're not sexual, but we are damn sure connected mentally. I always told you that scares me."

Terrance walked over. "Well what about it?" He asked while shutting my door.

"Nothing, it is just amazing to me the way we know each other so well." He started asking about the poetry again.

"Let's go to the club and listen to some poetry tonight. I mean, what have you got to lose? You've already lost him, he is gone like the birds." He started laughing.

I had to tell him again, "Shut the hell up, Terrance. Okay, what time?" He told me that it started at seven.

"Do you want me to pick you up?" Terrance asked me. I agreed and told him that seven was okay. I started the car and left for home.

CHAPTER TWENTY THREE

Decisions

When I arrived home, Melvin's empty spot of the driveway reminded me that he was gone out of town. I was still exhausted, so I didn't know why I made plans with Terrace. I still had five hours, so I got on the couch and was there for probably a second before I was knocked out due to the lack of sleep the night before. About five thirty the phone rang and woke me up. It was Melvin.

"Hey, baby, did I wake you?" This made my eyes spring open. I was so happy to hear from him. "I just wanted you to know that I have arrived and is checked into my room. What are you doing?"

"Well I was just waking from my nap. I had a hard day at work. I wanted to tell you about it earlier." We talked and I told him about how I felt. "Susan and Greg were working a number on me at work."

He listened patiently and told me not to worry about any of that. "I got you. I love you and that's all that matters. That's why I work so hard. It's for us, baby. One day I'm going to take you away and we'll live real good, you'll see. Not that we are not living good now, but soon you will be living like a queen, my queen." His words were so assuring. I hoped it meant we were going back to the closeness that we once shared. He told me that he had to turn in early and asked what I was going to do the rest of the night. As Melvin waited for an answer, I heard my cell phone going off in my purse. I knew it probably was Terrance about going to the club to listen to some poetry. I walked into the kitchen and told Melvin that I probably would be turning in also. We said our good nights and hung up. My eyes grew heavier and heavier by the minute, I was ready to turn in and really wasn't up to hanging out, so I called Terrance.

"Hey, buddy, I was just about to leave and-"

"Wait, Terrance, I can't go with you tonight."

His voice tumbled down and he started sounding downbeat. "What? I got my keys in my hand, ready to go. I even had a surprise with me. I was bringing Kenyetta along with me to meet you."

I started feeling as though I was letting him down. He was there for me today, and I felt as though I was bailing out on him. "I'm sorry, Terrance, I am just so tired, I thought that I would be able to go make it, but I just can't. I promise that I'll make it up to you next time promise, okay?"

Terrance was silent for a long time before he responded. "Okay, I understand go and get some rest. Don't worry about it, I'm about to go and pick up Kenyetta so we can get good seats." We said our goodnights then hung up. I felt really bad because the last thing that I ever wanted to do was hurt my buddy's feelings. I finally let go of the day's events and settled down for a good night sleep.

Two days had gone by and Melvin's absence was really haunting me. It showered me with a downpour of loneliness. And if that wasn't bad enough, I hadn't heard from Terrance, either. I looked at the clock and got ready for work. While at work, I was trying to get through a lot of stuff since it had been on my desk for two days. My duties at work had been going pretty well considering my status. I just kept a glimpse of hope with what Melvin told me the other night. All the things that bothered me about us had just melted away. I only looked toward the future from. I hoped that he would return by the end of the week. As I was thinking, Greg came into my office pushing a metal cart. It was filled with folders.

"Well, hey there, sunshine. I didn't want you to be lonely, so I brought these folders for you to input into the same system, but they must be filtered first so we will not be wasting any more time or money on good information." He was making me sick. He knew that I knew all about the information being inputted into proper channels to be more efficient for the company because I told him about it. I started thinking about the nerve of that punk ass mother fucker. I knew he was trying to get under my skin. I closed my eyes and asked him what he wanted me to do. He looked surprisingly shocked. "Well, you need to filter each entry and make sure that the companies we were dealing with had an updated account." Greg was enjoying every minute of it. I knew he liked drama, but I wouldn't give him any. My phone started ringing just in time for him to get his little skank behind out of my office.

The evening sky was outside my window, staring at me and guiding my thoughts into a lonely place. Mostly everyone had gone home. Why was I still there? My conscience told me and reminded me that I didn't have anybody waiting for me at home. I started thinking about Terrance and had grown tired of wondering about him, so I picked up the phone and dialed. I listened to three rings and was prepared to leave another message for him when he surprisingly picked up the phone.

"Hello." My heart was glad, at least my worries were put to the side.

"Terrance, where have you been? Why haven't you answered my calls? My spirit has broken from not connected with you."

He was silent for a little while, and then he finally spoke. "Yeah I'm sorry, Shante. I know it's been a couple of days, but when you didn't go to the poetry reading with me, I felt hurt. I wanted you to be there with me."

I was feeling puzzled because he had a date with him that night. "Why would you want me tagging along with you and your girl? I mean, that might have given her the wrong impression of me. Come on, Terrance, I'm a female and you don't know how we think. She would have interpreted a signal from that little action of me just being there as more than what it may have seemed."

Terrance sighed. "Come on now, Shante. We have been together in this friendship for too long. I wouldn't let no chicken head feel that way about my bud. Now come on. I really wanted you to be there that night."

Boy, it really must have meant a lot to him. "I'm so sorry." He acted as though it was killing him. "I can't stand for us to not have our daily interaction with each other."

Terrance told me that he felt the same, and then told me of another reading that was coming that Friday at six o'clock. He asked me if I had come up with any other poems. I told him that I was writing as I went along.

"Good, keep it up. One day you are going to have the courage to let everyone know how you have been really feeling inside." He was so encouraging, it was one of the best qualities in him. As soon as we hung up, Melvin called.

"Hey, baby, what's going on?" I was overjoyed to hear from

him. We talked for about thirty minutes and. I told him how much I missed him.

"I can't wait to see you Friday. We have so much more to make up for."

He had hesitation in his voice as he responded to me. "Yeah, baby, you know I love you. But, I won't be back until Friday night. The work here went over again. Some guys left and I was the only supervisor here. I had to stay longer to make sure everything was okay. But, hey, baby, keep the big picture in your mind that I was telling you about the other night. All of this is for a better future for both of us. Can you hold on until then?" I stubbornly told him okay. He blew me a kiss through the phone. "I love you," he said, then hung up.

CHAPTER TWENTY FOUR

When You Go Looking

I started thinking about what I had done so badly in the past to be getting such a short end of the stick. I couldn't think of anything. My nerves were so on edge that I had nervous energy, so I started cleaning up. Some people turned to biting their nails, some people start eating everything, and I, myself, started to clean. I glanced around the bedroom. Over in the corner I saw where I had started putting the laundry away but didn't finish. I went over and grabbed an armful of Melvin's shirts. As I was putting them in the dresser, a piece of paper underneath the bottom layer of his drawer was sticking out. I don't know why it drew my eyes to it. Melvin and I never disrespected each other's privacy, but for some reason, I was tempted to go further and see what was on that paper. I examined very carefully the position of it, because if I touched it, I wanted to replace it just as I had found it. I lifted the shirts on top of it and placed them to the side. What I saw was a folded sheet of paper with writing inside. When I lifted it up, a photograph fell from it facedown. I picked it up and turned it over. It was a photograph of a girl about the age of twenty two. Her breasts were exposed and she was seductively smiling, licking her tongue as to entice whomever it was she was taking the photo for. A ripple of hurt surged through my body like a rocket ship. The photo fell from my hand as tears started flowing down my face. My heart ached as I kept asking myself, "Why?" I finally unfolded the paper and it was a letter addressed to Melvin from Melinda.

Dear Melvin,

I was just writing to you a short note to thank you again for being so gentle and kind to me. You really did take good care of me as you promised. Thank you for keeping in consideration of this, especially this being my first time being introduced to the unknown. I'm so glad that I lucked up with someone who actually cares about the person themselves and not just the act itself.

Thank you so much

Love, Melinda

I cried even more after I read that note. I placed the letter and photo the way I found them. I went out into the kitchen and grabbed a bottle of Seagram's Gin, a bottle of cranberry juice, and started pouring my sorrows into the glass and letting my tears flow along with it. I knew in my heart that something was wrong, but I just couldn't put my finger on it and I still couldn't. I knew he was having an affair. I started asking myself, "Why?" I must not be enough for him. I couldn't provide him with a child. Maybe after that surgery so many years ago, I was left so bare inside that he really couldn't feel me. He may not get anything out of it. Was he just faking it all just to please me? He could be tired and have to get his now. I started feeling less than a woman at that point. I knew I fuck him the hardest and best I knew how. I let him fuck me most of the time, all ways he wanted. Maybe I didn't talk dirty enough to him. My mind was playing devil's advocate on me. It continued until I had emptied the bottle and passed out.

I woke up at three o'clock the next morning still bent over with my head on the kitchen table with a hell of a headache. It was still dark outside. I knew I probably wouldn't make it into work. The bathroom was my next destination for a wet washcloth to lie on my forehead. I got into my bed after that. I decided that I would be calling into the office for a sick day later that day. But, for now, I had to sleep off the hangover that I had. I closed the blinds because I knew in a few hours the sun would be reaching in to awaken me.

CHAPTER TWENTY FIVE

Mending Old Wounds

My phone was ringing and woke me up from a dead sleep. I managed to get one eye open to focus as I grabbed the phone. In a groggy, dead tone, I managed to speak.

"HELLLOOOOO. Where have you been, Shante? I really needed to talk to you the other day."

It was Sharise. I pushed the button and put her on speaker, and ran to the bathroom for some Excedrin. My hangover headache would not give up until I cried uncle. Sharise started going on, but it was different this time. She was talking about the birds and the bees, in other words, she was in love this week. Vance must have rocked her boat to no ends. It was only just two weeks ago that Sharise wanted his head on a platter from suspicions of him being unfaithful to her. She changed more than the seasons of the year. One minute she loved him, the next she wanted to kill him.

"Shante, what are you doing home? I called your office and they said that you were taking the day off. Are you feeling okay?" I told her that I just needed some serious me time. "What are you saying? I know my little sister don't need no time off. I thought your life was so perfect. How is your perfect husband, Melvin, doing?" She was being sarcastic so early in the morning, and the way I was feeling, I was not the one to be fucking with, sister or no sister.

"Look, Sharise, do you need something because I am not feeling so well this morning."

"Oh, it's like that now? I remember when we used to talk and just kick it, but ever since you moved out and away, got your little job, and got married, you have changed. And every time I mention Vance, you never want to hear it. Sometimes, Shante, I think you are jealous of me and Vance. And here lately, I know you think you are better than me. And back to me and Vance, I know you have always been jealous of us ever since we have been together and I know what happened at home, why you left so abruptly years ago, too. Vance told me how you used to beg for him ever since that night that you caught us, you couldn't stand it, could you? I know that you have always wished it were you on that sofa that night."

That girl was tripping. Was it me or wasn't it just the other day that Sharise was willing to think about changing her life for the better and get rid of that sleaze bag Vance? She was bringing up ancient history from so long ago. But, if that's how she wanted to go at it, I was ready to roll the dice. I felt as though the time had come for me to tell her the truth about her precious sweet Vance.

"Look, Sharise, I'm so sick and tired of you going through your little episodes of emotions. What the hell is wrong with you? I am one of little words. I love you and never wanted to hurt you, but it really hurts me when you believe all of the words from somebody who is not even your blood. Granted, I know that Vance is the father of your children and you now are permanently connected to him even more now than ever, but when I think about all of those years you believed him and took his side with so many of his lies that he's told you, it really hurts. I was always there when you went through occasional doubts about him. Those were your true signs, but you ignored them and pushed them to the back of your mind, and I never said a bad word about him. It's only when those thoughts and gut feelings resurfaced, then I could talk to you and I felt my true sister. But when you're like you are today, say things to hurt me, put me down with your cheap shots, I am going to finally tell you the truth. Vance is a motherfucking dog. I can't stand him most of the time. He makes my skin crawl. I can't tell you the times that he used to try and fuck me in the house and you were right there upstairs. It was worse when he moved in with us. I caught him trying to get away without anyone seeing him with some bitch he had brought home to fuck her in your bed. He had no idea that I had came home early that day. He had a woman, and brought her in your bed, and he fucked her. That's when he really got paranoid of me telling you. You used to take your medication, have a drink, and were knocked out. I am sorry that I was the one to tell you, but that's the person I have become. I held too much shit bottled up inside, apparently never to forget, but I stored it until I had to explode when provoked." Sharise had lit the fuse and I went. "He turned you against me because I would never put out. That's why I could never stand Vance all wrapped together in a nutshell. So, don't ever think that I was ever jealous, I was really feeling sorry for you and was mad as hell and wondered why my sister was so blind." Sharise was apparently shocked because she was quiet for several minutes after that. "I feel terrible saying these things you, but it is only the truth and I know it hurts to hear it, but being in the state of mind that you are in today, you are in absolute denial. I know that none of what I am telling you don't even matter to you, Sharise, because with you, it seems Vance's dick is thicker to you than your own blood."

"Fuck you, Shante. You are truly trippin'." The next thing in I heard in my ear was a slamming hang up without a goodbye. That hurt to no end. I hung up the phone and started gazing across my living room. My eye caught an old family portrait of Ma, Da, Sharise, and I that we had taken so many years ago. We were all so happy then. I wished that I could close my eyes and reopen them, only to be back in that very time for things to be back the way they used to be. That was really just wishful thinking, wishing they were still here.

Friday had finally arrived I was still at home due to me taking the rest of the week off. I waited for Melvin to give me a call but received nothing. I had no patience for anything. I picked up the phone and gave him a ring on his cell phone. The only thing I got was his answering service. I hung up and slammed the phone down. I sat there with an angel on one shoulder and the devil on the other, trying to decide which way to go. I picked up a pencil and started scribbling the lines that came to me.

If I hold onto my dreams
And promise to never let go
Will my efforts be rewarded?
Or will anybody ever know?
Don't criticize me when,
I stop along the way
There are lessons I must learn
Sometimes my heart will pay

I put those lines together with the poem I had not titled yet. I still was not finish with it, I knew it was not complete, but I felt good about it. I picked up the phone and called Terrance. "Hey, Shante, what's up?"

At first I was silent but then broke it. "Hey, Terrance, what time are you picking me up this evening?"

He told me at about five thirty, but when I thought about it, I told Terrance I would meet him there. I hung up and stared at my poem, still trying to think of a title. I wondered would I ever get the nerves to recite it. It still didn't feel quite finished to me. I knew that I would feel it in my heart when it was finished. I jumped in the shower, got dressed, and before leaving the bedroom, what I had found earlier in Melvin's dresser drawer was calling me. I went and pulled out the letter and picture from his whore. I could not believe that he had done that to me. I knew that I hadn't talked it over with him yet, but what could he possibly say to explain the photo and letter? I propped the photo right next to the thank you letter on his pillow. I headed for the car to go meet Terrance to relax and the club to hear some much needed words.

CHAPTER TWENTY SIX

Words Soothing My Soul

I pulled into the parking lot and spotted Terrance walking up to the car with some loud colored plaid tennis shoe on. I looked down and asked him, "Where and why?"

"Man, come on, Shante, this is the newest thing in Polo. They bad, ain't they?"

"Man you got that right. They are bad, not good at all."

"Oh come on, stop hating."

"Okay, I will as soon as you take those hideous looking shoes off."

We both fell out with laughter as we walked up to the entrance. Terrance looked over at me with his usual comforting smile as he opened the door for me. We walked into the club and followed the hostess to a table up front. I looked over in the corner and saw a table tucked away. I guess she read my mind and showed us to the corner table. Snappy jazz tunes filled the air. Terrance asked me what had been going on.

"Well, Terrance, let me tell you what the latest news is with me. You already know about that crazy bitch at work and all the drama she has given me." Terrance acknowledged that. A waitress came over and took our drink orders. I ordered a margarita, and Terrance had his usual gin and tonic. Terrance gave his undivided attention. I told him about Melvin's latest behavior and my suspicions of him messing around. Terrance stopped me and told me that I must be trippin'. Before Terrance could finish I held up my hand. "Look, I found a letter and photo under his clothes in his dresser drawer from some slut literally telling everything between the two of them." Our drinks had arrived and Terrance sipped on his. He seemed so deep in thought after what I had told him.

"When did all of this shit happen? You have been holding out on me. I thought we were tight like this." Terrance held up his fingers up intertwining them together. The MC came on stage to introduce the first poet. I told Terrance that we would talk after the show was over. Even though Melvin had really upset me, I still felt a little strange being out at night without him. I was going to try and relax.

The lights went dim and we heard, "Ladies and gentlemen, put your snapping fingers together and give Ebonette a warm welcome for showing us a picture of inside her mind." A spotlight came on to a very curvaceous, feminine figure sitting on a stool. A jazz piece from Peter White came on for her background and she began to recite her piece.

Don't tell me I'm too sexual
When I write of hot passion
I am her,
A black woman
With a mind to express my feelings
Don't tell me I'm too sympathetic
When I write about the children
I am her,
A black mother
With a mind that knows and cares
Don't tell me I'm a racist
When I write of realities
Believing all wounds must heal
For unity among all races
I am her
A black liberal
With a mind for worldly peace
Don't tell me I'm a sexist
Sometimes men are all the same
I am her
A black realist
I have a mind for honesty
My mind is filled with colors
Red, blue, yellow, and green
But the mystery of my mind
Is the greatest you've ever seen

I am her
A black woman
With a very powerful mind

The silence in the room was suddenly filled with the snapping of fingers, along with cheering and standing ovations. Terrance and I joined in. Her words were so powerful and that piece struck a nerve within me. I felt a buzz in my pocket because my phone was going off. I pulled it out and it was Melvin. How long had I been waiting for this moment for my husband to call me? Ironically, I thought that I would jump at that moment, but I guess that drink had calmed my nerves a little. I stared at the phone through three, four, five, and then silence. It stopped ringing, only to be replaced by a message that he left. Terrace looked at me.

"Who was that?"

"Melvin."

"What, and you didn't answer? He is going to whoop that ass."

I smiled. "Shut up, man."

"When Melvin finds out anything it's going to be some shit."

"Look, Terrance, have you been listening to anything that I've been telling you? That shit that I saw hidden in his dresser drawer, the letter and photo from his bitch posing in a sexual position specifically to him. I don't have to be a rocket scientist to figure this one out. "

Terrance looked at me and said, "If Melvin finds out anything, it's going to be shit hitting the fan."

I interrupted. "Look, Terrance, do you realize about a week has gone by since he had left town? He called me only a couple of times in the entire week that he has been gone. I think he's got some explaining to do before he tries to start any shit with me." I was curious about the message, so I dialed and listened.

"Shante, where in the hell are you at? And why have you been pulling things out of my dresser drawer? Call me as soon as you get this message because we need to talk. Call me back. I'm at home." He sounded as though he was agitated. I thought the nerve of him. It was in black and white. The message was clear. I'd been real stupid for years.

Terrance knew he had struck a nerve with me. "Okay, I'm sorry, Shante. I don't know where his fucking head is at. If I had a woman like you, I would treat you better than gold."

"Thank you, Terrance." He looked sincerely with his last comment. Terrance reached over and rubbed my hand across the table. Another poetess was introduced.

"Ladies and gentleman, let's give it up for Anita telling us about the better things in life." Finger snapping filled the air as the lights dimmed and the spotlight came on another figure sitting on a stool holding the mic.

I am held deep within your soul
I am a multitude of things
Yet invisible
Not showing myself until released
Your mind it controls my being
I am a heat ray soothed by a breeze
I am a the sun that settles in the evening
I am air being released from a balloon
I am a tooth being extracted
From pounding nerves
I am a radiator being bled from stem
I am a dry throat being quenched from thirst
Despite all the tensions that I represent
I'll let you see colors
The prettiest rainbow in your mind
The brightest that was ever revealed
In the sky of your imagination
I control the ocean waves deep within you
I represent you fully and whole
I am the orgasm of life

"Damn, that was deep, Shante. She was coming from a woman's view, but I was feeling her, it was making me understand." We both started laughing.

"You know what, Terrance, you're right." I drank the rest of my drink. I was feeling really relaxed, too. My troubles with Melvin were almost forgotten until I felt that buzz again in my side. It was Melvin again. That time I answered. "Hello."

Melvin yelled in the phone, "Shante, where the fuck are you? I've been calling and I know you heard me calling you on this damn phone. Why did you go through my shit in my drawer and left my stuff out on the bed?" I kept my cool and felt great from my margarita. I even snickered along with Terrance in the background. "Who are you with? I hear a motherfucking nigger in the background. Shante, Shante." He was started to bring me down with his bullshit.

"What do you want, Melvin? I'm out trying to figure things out in my head about you, wondering have I been a fool in this relationship and if I have, just for how long. It really upset me to find that shit with that photo and a letter of that bitch in your drawer. How long had that been going on?" There was a bit of silence, and then he started up again on his end.

"First of all, you had no right or business to go through my stuff. I would never invade your privacy. For as long as we have been together, I never have. And you know why, Shante? It's because I trust you enough not to do that. So why did you have to do this?" He was still trying to make me feel guilty and pin the whole thing on me.

"You know, Melvin, I'm too old for the motherfucking reverse psychology. You are not going to pin this one on me. True, we have been together long enough for honesty and trust, but you have broken that when you brought this shit into our relationship. Yes, I may have been wrong to invade your space, but you had this hidden because you didn't want me to find it. And I would not have seen it had it not been for the vibes that you have been giving off for so long of infidelity. I'm just feeling that there is something going on with you, Melvin. We are not the same like we used to be. Something is definitely missing from my life and it's you. You don't hold me the way you used to. You don't kiss me the way you used to. To sum it all up, you act as though you really don't want me anymore." Tears started streaming down my face. "Who is she, Melvin, who is she?"

He was silent for a few minutes. He finally broke his silence without answering my question. "Look, Shante, where are you? I need you to get your ass home now so we can talk about this." He hung up. Melvin left me staring across the table at Terrance with a blank expression.

"Shante, are you okay?" I put the phone back in my pocket. "Are you ready to go and handle your business? I think you should go and talk to him because I wouldn't want him to become any madder and anything worse could happen. Then, I would definitely have to step into the picture." Over on the stage they asked if anyone in the audience wanted to try their voice at open mic to try their virgin poetry on anyone. Terrance looked at me, "Well, are you ready to try your piece?" I told him no. "I better go home and face the music." Terrance got up, came over to my seat, and we walked out together to the car. I opened my car door, got in, and started the engine. Terrance came to my window, motioning me to roll it down.

"I want you to get it out of your head that you are the one that have to face the music. You have done nothing wrong. You have to just let him know that you are not completely blind and cripple. Don't let him turn and flip the script on you, turning everything around. Stay on him about what you have found. I know I shouldn't be telling you this, but always remember that women are from Venus and men are from Mars. We don't like to be caught stealing cookies from the cookie jar. Translation, if you walked in on a brother fucking someone with his dick in a woman, he will always stick with his story, it ain't me. Now if it was vice versa, he would have your ass waiting for the guillotine down in the dungeon for your number to be up, just like Queen Anne who lost her head. I know it's unfair, but it ain't no brothers who will admit anything. Stay strong, be careful, and if you need me just call me. I know it wouldn't be my place, but you are my best buddy, the best that anyone could ever have. I never want to lose you." I rolled the window up a bit and headed for home.

CHAPTER TWENTY SEVEN

Guilt Mixed With Paranoia Is A Deadly Combination

I pulled up to the house and the porch light was on. I gave a heavy sigh and headed up the driveway. When I reached the front door, I put my key in the lock, but didn't get a chance to turn it because Melvin snatched the door open with my key still in the lock. I walked in and I could still see the fiery look in his eyes. I had to remember that tip that Terrance had given me. 'Remember he is just mad because he has been found out.' As I walked in, Melvin took the keys out the door and slammed it close. I jumped from the noise. We stared at each other for awhile, and then Melvin started.

"What the hell has gotten into you? First of all, where have you been? You knew I was coming back tonight and you were not even here for me. I hope you're not fucking around on me because if I found out, I'm going to kill your ass. So I'm going to ask you again, where the fuck was you?"

I looked at him surprisingly. Out of all of these years of being together, he has the nerve to ask about my whereabouts. "Melvin, what is wrong with you? You act as though---------" he cut me off.

"You know that you are fucking around on me. You can't answer this simple question of your whereabouts tonight. I'm off working really hard for us and you can't keep your ass at home until I get back."

My head was spinning. I didn't know how the situation turned three hundred and sixty degrees on me. It definitely felt as though I was in the *Twilight Zone,* modern day style. "Melvin, why are you getting off the subject of what's going on here? What was that letter and photo about that I found in your dresser drawer?"

Our yelling had escalated and either of us was listening to the other. He was wearing me down. I walked away and went to get washed up for the night. I closed the bathroom door with him on the other side still asking me who I was with. I turned on the water, closed my eyes, and thought about the poem I just heard, *The Better Things In Life*. I definitely was feeling it. I turned the water off when I was finished and opened the door, and Melvin stood there with my phone gave it to me.

"While you were in the bathroom, I guess Terrance is your punk ass boyfriend. He just called and asked for you."

When he accused me of that it scared the shit out of me. He didn't know about my Terrance. "Why were you answering my phone? That was in my purse?"

"Oh, you mean like you went in my shit? Do you feel it's wrong now that I caught up with your lying ass? Who is this fucking Terrance?" Melvin grabbed my shoulder, shaking my small frame, trying to get an answer.

"He is just a friend."

"Well, why did he call you at this time of night? It seems like a convenience he called as soon as you get in the house tonight."

I started crying uncontrollable. I guess I didn't do well on this because I was letting him turn everything around on me. Melvin came over to me and put his hand on my back. He rubbed it in efforts to comfort me. I calmed down.

"Okay, Melvin, let's stop all of this yelling. It's not fair for you to keep badgering me like this. I told you I was not and never have messed around on you. I answered your question, now how about you being fair and answer mine. Who is that chick in the photo, and what is that letter about that she wrote?"

"Look what you found in my dresser drawer have been in there for a long time. I had even forgotten that it was even there. Now, I hope that you remembered that I had moved into this place before we were married. This was a bachelor pad. I did know other girls before you. I am not messing around on you. Now, what about this mother fucking Terrance? Who is he and why have you never talked about him?"

"Look, Melvin, Terrance is just somebody that gave me information on a spot where I could go and listen to some local poets. Sometimes when you go on your business trips, I write to keep myself busy. I barely know him. When I left the poetry club, he saw me to my car. He was just being a gentleman, that's all."

"Okay, Shante, if it ain't all of that, then why did he call you on your cell phone?"

Damn he was jamming me up real good. *Think fast, Shante.* "Well, he said he could give me the name of some poets that are very good and when he got their numbers, he would give me a call to pass it on. I guess he got their numbers."

He looked at me and said, "When did you start this writing shit anyway?"

I went and grabbed my writing pad with all that I have ever written and handed it to him. "See, look all of this I made up and put into poetry. I went to the club to recite but couldn't get my nerves up. It would be nice if you were there to cheer me on. It's one in particular that I am working on, would you like to hear it. It starts with like this, a satisfied—"

"Look, I don't want to hear none of this shit. I think that you are lying to me, just don't let me find out, Shante." He slammed my pad on the table without even looking at it and went into the kitchen and grabbed a beer from the refrigerator. I was going to let it go. "Is there anything in here to eat? Oh wait, I guess not since you had to go and listen and speak that poetry shit of yours, or so you say. You should have got up and told them how you don't stay home anymore and take care of me when I get home."

Now he was starting to get sarcastic on me. I just ignored the remarks, along with my hurt feelings of his showing no interest in anything that I've done. I went to the kitchen and grabbed something for him to eat. It was amazing how you could argue with someone and in minutes trust them to cook your food. I knew that this was the devil talking in my head, but I knew how to ignore it and still try to be nice. Melvin was sitting in front of the television in his favorite lazy boy chair. I came up behind him, embraced his neck, and I handed him a sandwich that I made for him. I still was upset, but I was trying to let it go. I looked at the time and tried to get myself ready for bed. After I gave him his dinner, I still felt like there was a sheet of ice between us, but I figured when he came to bed he would try and melt it and by tomorrow it would all be a bad dream.

CHAPTER TWENTY EIGHT

Strange Behavior

I got into the bedroom and sprayed on Vera Wang that Melvin loved me to wear along with a sexy red teddy that I had just bought. I'd had been waiting for this a long time. I wanted to put all my negative feelings away. When Melvin came in, he smiled and gave me a kiss on my cheek. He came over to me and caressed my shoulder. He stood me up, turned me around, and bent me over on the side of the bed where he tenderly laced kisses down my back. The anticipation of me wanting him so badly was highly intensified at that moment, and then Melvin reached over and turned out the light. He reached down and caressed my breast from underneath.

"Oh, baby, I've been waiting for this so long."

"Show me how bad you want it. Tell me." Melvin caught me off guard with that. "I'm going to make you feel like a hot ass slut. Would you like that? I need to make you feel like a satisfied black woman as you wrote about." He reached down and played with my clit until it was throbbing for him. "Baby, tell me what you want, and Daddy will give it to you."

I whimpered and quietly said, "You."

He wouldn't let that pass. "What? I can't hear you, tell me again."

"You," I said it louder, but that still wasn't loud enough for him.

"Okay, Daddy is going to give it to you, but first you got to tell Daddy where you want him to put it, inside your hot pussy or this steamy, virgin ass?" He smacked my left ass cheek as he said that. "Daddy's not going to hurt you either way, it's going to make you feel so good that you're going to cream all over me." His breathing was erratic and quite frankly, he was scaring me. My pleasure was quickly turned a little to fear. I stopped my movements with him. I wanted him to calm down. "What's wrong?" he asked with heavy breathing. I shifted, trying to get from under him. He stopped and moved from over top of me.

I got up and held my stomach. "Melvin, I'm sorry, it feels as though I'm coming on." I went to the bathroom and closed the door. I felt as though he was a different person, he was not my Melvin. I thought to myself, *Think, think fast.* I reached down into the cabinet under the sink, pulled out a tampon, and coated it with some KY Jelly.

Melvin yelled from the other side of the door. "Hey, Shante, hurry up and get your hot ass out here."

"Okay, but I'm afraid Mary, my visitor, has come to see me."

He got quiet. "Well, we can bring her along with us on our travels. It may be a little messy, but I don't mind."

I opened the door. "No, not this time, besides, my stomach is started to cramp. I'm sorry."

We got in the bed for the night. Melvin reached down under the covers and touched me between my legs. He was so horny, but he felt the string and was convinced to just leave me alone for awhile. I knew something has changed about him. He had never done anything like that before. I was glad I thought of the old period trick. That would at least buy me some time to think and sort things out.

CHAPTER TWENTY NINE

Mediator

The next day at work, I was swamped with the usual workload that Greg had given me. I knew he was doing it to annoy me, but he was not going to have any fun because this fish wasn't biting. I looked out my office window and I saw him glance in at me. He looked so disappointed. Well, it would have to be that way because I had got a lot on my mind. My phone rang.

"Dave and Donavan, Shante Brenin speaking."

"Okay, so when were you going to give a brother a call?"

"Hey, man, I had to recoup from last night travels from the far end of that *Twilight Zone*."

"What happened? Did you use my rules and techniques, or did you sucker like I know he wanted you to?"

I got up and closed my office door so I could tell Terrance all about last night's events. "First of all, Terrance, I want to apologize for Melvin's answering my phone last night when you called."

Terrance was quiet for a moment, and then finally broke it. "What are you talking about? I never talked to Melvin last night. Oh, wait a minute. I did call you, but your message service came on. Man, he suckered you. Let me guess, he saw my name when I called and he told you that we had a conversation last night. I know his next move was probably to have you spill your guts about me. Am I right?"

"Yeah, but."

"Damn, girl, he must have had you so nervous you gave all the information on me, right? Now that I am looking at the whole picture, I see now what happened. He saw my name on your phone last night. He never talked to me, but used it against you in the argument just to get information from you. And in this entire time, I know you forgot all the rules I had told you about."

"Boy, I guess I was suckered by Melvin last night." I told Terrance about Melvin's behavior.

"Shante, I told you the man wanted you. I know you had to give it up."

"No, Terrance, that's the most ironic thing about this whole situation. All of this time, it didn't happen. My life has been on such a rollercoaster for the past months, I don't know if I am coming or going. I missed him so much only a few weeks ago. We couldn't seem to get enough from each other. Then all of a sudden, things started strangely and quickly changing. I keep those suspicious feeling about him all the time like I was telling you at the club. I try to dismiss them, but it's getter harder to do. All of those clues I have been finding around the house. And the way he acted the last night with me so strongly, it has scared me to death, so much that I had to lie about being on my period so he wouldn't touch me. He has come back home so out of character."

Terrance laughed. "You know that little stunt you pulled last night was wild. Your ass only has four more days to be on your phantom period. And what about your real period when it does come, how are you going to explain that your still bleeding? I tell you, girl, when you tell one bloody lie it leads to another one." He laughed for awhile with that one. "I mean maybe he just really wanted you. You haven't given it up for awhile. Come on now, Shante, it's your husband, Melvin."

"I know, but he feels like a stranger." "

Well, let's talk later. I got to get back to my good government job here at this treasury department." We then hung up.

I prepared the rest of my assignments at my desk and went to deliver them to Greg's ass. He wasn't in his office and I was relieved that I didn't have to deal with him for a moment. The rest of the day went by with no negative incidences and I was finally on my way home. My phone rang, I pressed the speaker, and it was Melvin.

"Hey, baby, what you up to?"

"Oh, I'm on my way home. What about you?"

"Oh nothing, I'm just waiting for you to get here. I got a big surprise waiting for you when you get here. Are you feeling better?"

God he was totally different from what he was yesterday. I mean, he had gone from being furious with me, to a scary bedroom freak, to the loving, caring husband that I was used to. "Okay I'll be there soon, I love you."

"Love you." We hung up.

Maybe he was just having a bad day. I started to think that maybe I should have been there for him. I pushed on the gas at the green light and was off for home.

CHAPTER THIRTY

Trying To Smooth Things Over

When I pulled into the driveway, I spotted David's car. I walked in and they all were sitting in the living room, shooting the breeze, drinking beer, and laughing. "Hey, here goes my baby," Melvin bellowed out. David had a different girl sitting in his lap, playing in his neatly shaped up goatee. He smiled and excused little missy off his lap and gave me a hug.

"Hey, girl, you are looking good as usual. I want to introduce you to the lady that I think I'm going to marry. This is Desiree."

I smiled. "Hello, Desiree, it's a pleasure to meet you."

Melvin told me to help him in the kitchen. I followed him and he whispered to me. "Hey, you know David, it seems like he changes women like underwear."

"Where is Lucinda, I believe her name was?" I asked.

"I don't know, I just go with the flow with him. Don't ask any questions." We both laughed.

"Melvin, I'm going to get out of these clothes, freshen up, and will see you all shortly."

When I finished getting comfortable, I joined them and we all had a good time, but that time we didn't stay up to late. When they left Melvin put his big surprise on me. "Baby, I wanted to surprise you with this."

He handed me an envelope. When I looked inside there were two plane tickets and hotel reservations to stay at an all exclusive hotel in the Cayman Islands, booked for three weeks from now. I screamed and grabbed him, and planted a much missed and needed kiss. I was so in the caught up in a momentarily happiness that everything negative that had happened between Melvin and I had been put in a back of my mind. I felt that he was pleased again with life, and if he was pleased I was right along with him. Every time Melvin brought happiness into my life, all the sadness was over shadowed and forgotten. I was slowly turning into my sister Sharise, living life with blinders on and not seeing it for what it really was. He wanted us to get away to sort and melt that stress we had away. He walked over to me smiling from ear to ear. I ran and looked at the calendar and had to plan what days I would be taking off from work.

When Melvin came back over to me, he looked at me. "Damn, I wish you was not on, I want you so bad."

I looked at him and thought I saw my old Melvin back. I whispered in his ear, "Baby, I got a surprise for you, too. That was a false alarm last night. My stomach felt so much better today. And there was only a spot last night. It wasn't time anyway. Maybe I was just stressed out. "

Melvin's eye glowed. "Damn, this must be my lucky night." He had did a three sixty on me. He looked into my eyes and told me again, "I've been waiting for so long." Melvin slid my clothes off just as I was taking his off. He didn't attack me, he only showed gentleness with his touches. He cascaded my body from my forehead all the way down to my toes with gentle kisses. He got back to eye level with me and told me he loved me. I felt his rod of pleasure wedging in between us, knocking for my doormat of wetness to welcome him. I was melting with a desire to love him. I managed to get up and pushed him down on his back. "Hey, I guess you're taking charge of this situation," he said.

I slid my wetness all over his stiff pole to make it easy for him to invade every inch of it into my love tunnel. I grabbed him and directed him inside me. He moaned with pleasure as well as I did. Our rhythm was perfectly in sync as I bounced and succumbed down on him. He grabbed my hips and fucked me absolutely out of my mind. His rhythm got more intense, his breathing got shallower, and I moaned while calling his name out as he continued to make me have multiple orgasms on top of multiple orgasms. He reached his height and tried to pull out as to prolong his stiffness, but my pussy overruled and gripped him so tight he could not maintain it any longer. He let out a roar as he called my name and came within me. I collapse on top of him. We both were trying to catch our breath as we smiled at each other.

It was late when the phone rang and caught us both still butt naked and sleepy from our latest love making up session. I looked at the clock and it was twelve 'o clock. "Heeeellloo," I answered in a sleepy greeting.

"Hey, Shante, I'm sorry to wake you, but I need to speak with my brother." It was David. He sounded as though he was in a panicked state. I reached over and shoved Melvin a little.

"Melvin, Melvin, wake up, the phone is for you."

"Whhaat, What is it?" Melvin was trying to open his eyes, still drugged from our love making events just a few hours ago. He finally took the phone as he rubbed the sleep from his eyes. "Hello. What? Where are you? Damn it, David, I'll come this time, but you are going to have to be more careful." He hung up. "Shit, sometimes David will do some of the dumbest shit, then he will inconvenience anybody to bail him out of these situations that he has gotten himself into." Melvin sat up rubbing his head. I asked him what had happened. "Well my stupid ass brother has got himself locked up in New York. Now he needs someone to bail him out. I have to go over to his house, get his bankcard, and withdraw the money from his account. I am not offering to use my money because he probably will never pay it back."

"What did he do? And what is he doing in New York?"

"Well, he said he was visiting a friend up there. They went up last night after they left here. They had drinks and went out looking and cruising for some girls. They hooked up with some tricks, and then they ripped them off. The hookers called the police and told them that David and his friends had ripped them off."

"Man, you know I was really started to like David. The longer I knew him, he is acting more like a dog. I used to think more of him than that." Melvin sat the clock for three a.m. Poor baby I knew he was tired, but he was loyal to a lot of people. That was one reason why I loved him so much. Melvin turned off the light and we both fell back into our slumber.

My alarm clock was going was going off at seven. I reached over for Melvin and he was already up. I called out to him and there was no answer. I sat up rubbing my eyes and remembered that he had left early heading up for New York to help David. I jumped in the shower and get ready for work.

While sitting in traffic, I turned on my Ledisi CD and felt empowered as I jammed to her poetic jams on my way to work. I was at a red light I closed my eyes as thought about last night. I could still feel

Melvin pounding in me until a car horn blew from behind me. The driver stuck his head out the window.

"Okay, maybe you would like to go to work this morning perhaps."

I motioned my hand outside my window going up and down. "Go on over the top asshole." He gave one longer honk as he got around me and sped off. It didn't bother me because mentally I was feeling good. "Can't a girl have aftershocks from still feeling her man up in her? Damn, I got to shake this feeling by the time I get to work."

Finally, I was opening my office door. I could hear my phone ringing off the hook. I rushed trying to get my key in and by the time I got to it, the ringing had stopped. I had several messages waiting to be played. I grabbed my pen, picked up the phone, put my password in, and started listening and writing my messages down. The first message was from a client that wanted me to set up an account from her. I wrote down her information so I could call her back. The next one was from Greg asking me about, I pushed the button before I could even hear him even ask me for whatever. I chucked to myself, "Oops, my hand slipped." That was a bad thing to do. Next was Sharise, who I didn't expect to hear from her for at least another two weeks. It was always a pattern when she and I argued. She always got steamed with me from the beginning of the argument, and in about two weeks she'd calm down. I'd call her back. "Hey, buddy, what's up. Like that, you didn't call me last night. Are you okay, or do I have to come over there and bust things up?" Terrance chuckled after his remark. I would get back to him after I got squared away. The next message had no name or telephone number, I only heard a woman's voice. "I've got to tell you that," then the line went blank. I figured somebody had the wrong number.

My mind drifted off to my vacation. I looked at the calendar and figured out my leave, then requested it in the leave system for Susan to approve. I couldn't wait for the three weeks to go by. I was so excited. My next task was to return all my calls promptly, so I called the potential client back and set up an account up for her. I looked on my list and scratched out the next name which was Greg's. I picked up the phone and called Sharise next to see if she was alright. "Sharise, hey, baby, are you okay?"

Sharise was sobbing. "Shante, he didn't come home at all last night. I know he is out with some slut."

"Sharise, calm down. Oh you know that I love you and it kills me to know that you are always going on a rollercoaster ride with Vance. You got three kids with him. Why don't you just leave him?"

She came back on me strong, "And what do you suggest that I do then?"

"He should be taking care of you and the kids with support since you quit your job years ago. I just want to see you to be happy for a change. You deserve it."

Sharise got quiet. "You know, Shante, I know that you're right about things. I know I've said this before, but one day I'm going to do the right thing, it's just that I'm scared and don't know how to start over and make it on my own. It's been so long."

"I know but I can help you with a new start. I always told you that you would not be alone. Maybe we can look and set up some interviews for you. But whatever you do, don't tell Vance about anything you are planning. All he is going to do is knock you down and discourage you. Just try to do your thing quietly." We hung up and I had to call my buddy after that.

I dialed Terrance because I knew I would feel uplifted after talking him. He answered with, "I mean, who is this stranger is calling my line? This phone is strictly for buddies only."

"Come on, Terrance, it hasn't been that long. I just talked to you yesterday. You have gotten to be so spoiled." I chuckled.

"I don't know, do I know you, Miss?" He was always joking around, but that's what made me love him as my buddy. I told Terrance about Melvin and I going away to the Cayman Islands. I was so excited. "Man, he really worked some magic on you. Well, I'm glad that things are working out for you. Look, I got to go deal with some customers, I'll l talk to you later."

After that, I worked and got a good amount done. When lunch came I decide to call Melvin. When he answered, he was in good great spirits considering what had happened with David last night. He said that everything was taking care of and for me not to worry. He told me he was going to come back tomorrow.

"Hey, baby, I want you to go into my savings and pull some money for you to go shopping with for the trip. Spend as much as you want. And remember, when you do that, remember this is what I work so hard for." That really made my day. I hadn't been shopping in quite awhile and I felt I was due for a little spree.

When I left work, I pulled up in the bank driveway. I put the bank card in and asked a balance first. When I looked at the slip the balance was $480,000. My eyes so wide from what I was seeing, I couldn't believe it. It had to be a mistake. I pulled around and parked my car, then rushed in and stood impatiently in line. When my turn finally came up, I ran up to the teller, showed my ID, and gave her the bank card. "Excuse me, but I think there has been a mistake on my husband's account. Is this amount correct?"

The teller went into the account and said, "Yes, Mrs. Brenin is there a problem?"

I guess that was what he was talking about what he was working so hard for. I withdrew $2,000.00 and was walking out of the bank as though I had just won the lottery. I was so hyped up as I drove from the bank. The money had blindsided me until nothing mattered to me anymore. I was just happy with the whole situation. I called Angie and asked her if she wanted to go on a shopping spree.

"Angie how about it, you want to shop until we drop? Let's go to Annapolis Mall. The sky's the limit. I'll even break you off a little summthin' summthin'. Just come and go shopping with me."

"Okay, girl, you ain't got to ask me twice."

"Let's go tomorrow."

"Okay, I'll be at your house."

I hung up with a bigger smile on my face. Every guy that passed by looked at me and thought I was smiling just for them it felt so good, I didn't let them think any different. I wanted everybody to feel as happy as I was.

When the next evening arrived, Angie and I were killing the mall. We had bought so much we had had to make two trips to the car. "Man, this is how it feels to shop until you drop," Angie exhaustedly said. We spotted an Italian café not far from the mall. We went in and cooled our feet while we ordered some lunch. The entire time we sat at the table we discussed the trip. "I'm so jealous, girl, I wish it was me going over to the Islands with me man. You are so lucky."

"Girl, I can hardly believe it myself. Pinch me to see if it is." Angie reached over and pinched me. "Oh, Angie, it is just a figure of speech you know." We started laughing and our food came out.

CHAPTER THIRTY ONE

Feeling Happy

It was finally here, I was on my way to the Islands. While on the plane, I drifted off into a slumber, dreaming of the photos that I had just seen in a magazine of the Islands. The plane touched down at six thirty in the evening. Melvin turned to me and nudged me out of my nap. "Baby, wake up, we're finally here." I opened my eyes to focus, and like a child in a candy store, I excitedly looked out the window to see all I could see. The seatbelt light went off, giving all of us the okay to get up and leave the plane. When we finally made our way to the door, the warm air greeted us as we walked down the steps of the plane. We made our way to get our luggage, and then found ourselves riding with another couple on a water taxi. They introduced themselves as Bobby and Anita Brown, a very friendly couple. We found it such a coincidence that we were staying at the same resort.

As we pulled up, the mere sight of the place took my breath away with its beauty. I had never seen anything like it in person. The lobby was like something out of a magazine. The flowers, paintings, plants, and waterfalls were spectacular. The staff was so friendly. Everything was in perfect order, no problems. Anita and I both looked in awe as Melvin and Bobby took care of everything at the front desk. While Melvin confirmed and took care of all the monetary portion of our trip, another clerk was telling us everything the hotel and about all of the Island activities that were offered to us. Next, we were escorted to the seventh floor. The Browns were being escorted at the same time to the very room next door. Anita and I were all smiles.

"Alright, I guess you all will be our hanging buddies," Bobby shouted out.

I shoved Melvin on his side. "Honey, I thought this trip was about just the two of us."

Melvin looked at me and said, "Come on, babe, it's nothing

wrong with being a little friendly. Besides, you know I have never been stuck up, and they are right next door."

When the door was opened to our suite, I placed my hand over my mouth in amazement of the beautiful breathtaking room that I stood in. There was a granite miniature waterfall slab near the front door. The colors were perfectly coordinated with the themes of paradise. There was a sixty inch flat screen television that hung in the front room in front of the sofa. Toward the back was a bar stocked with all the drinks; alcoholic, non alcoholic, and juices as well. As you went further back, there was the most gorgeous bedroom that was fit for a king and queen. The ceiling fan had blades made in the shape of leaves, and the ceiling was covered in mirrors. The bathroom had marble everywhere. There was a sit down shower and a heart shaped tub. When I walked toward the glass doors toward the outside balcony, it had the most beautiful view of the ocean and the white, sandy beach. I saw couples walking hand in hand everywhere. I grabbed Melvin around his neck so hard.

"Thank you so much for this. I love you so much."

"Okay, Shante, is you okay with the room?" he asked.

"Are you kidding, I love every inch of this room."

He reached down and kissed me. "Are you ready for the beach?"

"Yeah, baby, just let me go freshen up and change into my bathing suit." I went and glamorized myself. I looked in the mirror at my two piece bikini. I must say that I was wearing that itsy bitsy, I hoped he liked it. I walked out into the room looking fierce when Melvin looked he started drooling.

"Oh no, baby, you got too much of my ass showing off in that. That's mine. I don't know if I want everybody looking at what I got." He laughed. He was already in his swimming trunks. He looked at me again. "Damn." When I looked down at his shorts, his manhood was trying to emerge out. He came over to me and pulled on the strings on each side of my hips. The bottom of my bikini fell to the floor.

"Come on now, baby, I want to go and get wet."

He looked at me as he stroked his rod. "Oh, you are going to get wet in just a minute, believe me. " He planted his mouth on mine and laid me on top the bed and ravished me.

After a second time of freshening up, I came back out in the front room. Melvin started tapping me with the beach towel and I was running from him; we were acting like two young teenagers. Before we could open the door there was a knock. When we opened it, there stood our new friends from next door.

"Hey, we hope we're not interrupting, but we just wanted to know if you guys wanted to join us for dinner," Bobby asked.

Melvin told him that we were just about to do the same thing. They laughed so we all left and went to eat at The Seafood Delight Restaurant. We all were getting acquainted. Bobby and Anita were from Jacksonville, Florida. "We are here for a much needed and deserved vacation from our travel agency that we run." Bobby was proudly talking about their business, in fact, they went on and on most of the night until I had to fake a headache just so that Melvin and I could escape them for the night. I hoped that they would not bother us too much during the week.

On the way back, Melvin and I enjoyed the sand under our feet as we walked close to the edge of the water as the waves moved in close to the shore. Melvin turned me around and melted a loving kiss on my lips. "Damn, let's go back to our room to make love the rest of the night." I had no objections as we walked back into the hotel for the night.

A nice wonderful breeze accompanied with the sun was lightly touching upon my skin that came in from the open double doors from our balcony. It was telling me to wake up and enjoy another glamorous day on the Island. Melvin and I were both naked, sprawled across our King sized delight, resting up from our wild evening and night of hot passion. I smiled as a rose up. Melvin didn't even hear me. I wanted him to rest because I knew that he was drained. I turned on the coffee maker, then went into the shower and let the water fall down and dance on my skin. It felt so good. When I finished, I toweled dried and put a towel around my head, then headed for the freshly brewed coffee. I poured me a cup then went outside, sat in a lounge chair and soaked in the sun. I heard my cell ringing from my purse inside. Damn, I was having such a good time I forgot to call Sharise and let her know that we had arrived yesterday. I dashed off to get the phone so I could call her. Just as I picked it up it rang in my hand.

"Hello." There was hesitation, and then the same voice on the phone was there.

"Look, Mrs. Brenin, you've got to believe me."

"Who is this and why do you keep?"

Melvin had walked up and surprised me. He took the phone. "Hello, who the fuck is this?" I figured the person hung up when they heard Melvin. "Baby, you know what? I'm going to get the phone number changed. It doesn't make sense for some sick ass person to be ruining your relaxing fun time. I will take care of it when we get back to the states." He kissed my forehead. "Well, you've got coffee going on. I see those Danishes over there too. Mmmm." He went over poured a cup of coffee and grabbed a doughnut.

That was a weird thing for him to just pop up like that. My mind wanted to wonder more about that little incident, but as usual, I kicked it out and joined Melvin on the balcony. He reached over with that look in his eye. "Come on, Melvin, let's have more of that for this afternoon. Today, I would like to get started with some activities." I went and grabbed the book they had given to us the day before when we checked in. I flipped to the pages that I had marked. I pointed to the sailing activity and Melvin looked at it.

"Hey, are you serious? I don't know how to sail no boat."

I laughed and him. It was a large boat. "You can even see inside the ocean. It has a glass bottom. It's large with other people. It's like a tour. Come on, Melvin. We will have to make a quick reservation to save us spots for ten. Come on," I begged.

"Ok, damn, woman. Go ahead and make the reservation."

I grabbed him. "Thank you so much baby.

"Get ready, we have just enough time to grab a little to eat, then we can meet right downstairs." Melvin went to go get dressed. I put on a black swimsuit and wrapped my sarong around me. I picked the perfect sandals to go along with the outfit. We went downstairs to grab a bit to eat. While I went for the toast, Bobby and Anita were there.

"Well, what's up, neighbors?" Bobby yelled out. Man, it looked like we would be seeing them everywhere we went.

Melvin started smiling. "Hey, man, what's up?" They gave each other dap.

Anita came up to me. "Good morning. How are you doing, girl?"

"I'm okay."

They sat at our table. Melvin announced that we were getting ready to sail on the boat and Bobby started laughing. "Get the fuck out of here. We are going on that same sail. I think brilliant minds thin alike," he bellowed out, laughing with his food showing.

He was starting to irk the hell out of me. It didn't seem like Melvin and I would get a moment alone on the trip. Was I the only one thinking like this because Melvin seemed as though he didn't mind. I was wondering was I being selfish or was I being stuck up. I didn't think so; I just wanted some time alone with my man.

Twenty people were on the sail boat as the tour got started. Melvin hugged on me while Bobby and Anita were right beside us doing the same. Bobby pulled out his camera and started snapping pictures of us. "Come on, baby, these will be reach nice to show when we get home," Melvin said. He was really enjoying himself, so I posed with him. Then, Anita wanted the two of us to take pictures. Then before you knew it, we all were taken pictures together, having a good time. The view from the boat was beautiful. I felt like I really didn't want to leave.

After the ride, Melvin and I started a nice walk on the beach. I was really surprised that Anita and Bobby didn't tag along that time. We went to a nice place that served delicacies of the Island. When the waiter came, Melvin went to use the restroom so I ordered a chicken Caesar salad and a wonderful fruit salad. I knew he was going to protest. It was probably to light for him, but I wanted us to eat light for more activities. The waiter left two glasses of passion juice and Melvin came back he sat down. "Man, it's real nice in the men's room, clean as ever." He looked at the passion juice. "Oh they brought the drinks, did he come over for our orders yet?"

"Baby, I took care of that."

"Okay good, you ask about my fried chicken?"

"No, Melvin, it's a surprise. Just relax and they will bring you some food. You know you shouldn't be all that hungry anyway. I mean, we did have a little breakfast."

"What, that little stuff we ate? Now come on, don't you want me to gain my strength for you tonight, baby?" Melvin laughed.

"Now look, baby, you will have plenty of time to chow down. Tonight you can go for it. You can have you a juicy steak or something like that, okay?"

Melvin smiled and said, "Ummm," but before he could finish, our lunch had come out. His eyes looked at the salad and fruit. "What the—Shante? Do I look like a rabbit to you?"

The waiter placed our food down and smiled. "Is everything okay?"

"Yes, yes, he will be alright. Come on now, you spoiled baby. I told you tonight you can get you a nice, juicy steak."

Melvin grunted, "Okay," as he started eating his Caesar salad. The rest of the day we spent time horseback riding, and then we headed back to the hotel to rest from our exhausted day.

Back at the hotel, I called Sharise. It rang three times before Troy, my nephew, answered. "Hello."

"Hey, baby, where is your mama? This is auntie Shante."

"Hey, Auntie Shante, mama is downstairs with daddy, hold on." Troy went and got Sharise and it took like five minutes. What in the world could she be doing?

Finally, she came to the phone, and almost in a whisper she said, "Hello." I could barely hear her.

"Sharise, it's me, Shante. I know you have been wondering why I haven't called."

She took her time responding to me. Then she finally said, "No, I've been busy." She was talking so softly as though she didn't want anyone to hear her. "Look, Shante, I will call you back, okay? I promise, I just can't talk right now." Then, she hung up.

"Hello?" She really did hang up. Oh well, she must was in the middle of something very important. I was sure she would call back. I went in the room and Melvin was flipping through the T.V. channels. He placed his hand on my thigh, but he drifted off into sleep with me following right behind him. We left the television on to watch us.

Not surprisingly, a knock at the door that startled and woke both of us up. It was Bobby and Anita. I gave a tired sigh and started to get up, but Melvin pulled me back and placed his finger over his lip. "Shhhh, don't make too much noise." I couldn't believe Melvin didn't want to be bothered with them.

We then heard them talking. "Maybe they have left early."

Then Bobby said, "Come on, maybe we will see them outside somewhere." The knocking stopped.

Melvin laughed and started tickling me as he pulled the covers over us. "Baby, it's something."

"What?" I asked.

He looked around. "Damn, a hard boner that is waiting for you to wrap him and make it feel good. Come here, you." He wrapped his arms around me and made the hottest love to me until I was paralyzed from cumming so much.

Our stay was pretty much over. Boy, how time flies when you are having fun. We had avoided Bobby and Anita for about three days. It was easy, but I pretty much knew that they heard us through the walls. I should be put in the *Guinness Book of Records* with a cum record. I felt like I was truly in paradise. Melvin got up early to go get a paper in the lobby and I told him I was going to relax in the Jacuzzi. I ran the water and put some bath salts to soothe me. I filled the tub up and slipped in, relaxing all of my overworked muscles. When Melvin came back I had been in the tub for about thirty minutes.

He peeked in. "Hey, babe, how you feeling?"

"The second best to what you have made me feel this week. What's up?"

"Hey, I ran into Bobby while I was downstairs." Oh God, what was he about to tell me. We had managed to dodge them for three days and we only had a couple to go. "He started asking me if they had got on our nerves. He kind of got me on the spot. Man, I didn't want to hurt their feelings, so I told him no. He asked me about us going tonight with them on a booze cruise. So, I told him that we would go. Is that okay?"

"Well, Melvin, if that would make you happy, then I guess we can go."

The closer we walked up to the boat, we started hearing the calypso music filling the air with majestic tunes. We met up with Anita and Bobby who were standing in the front waiting. Bobby threw his hand up so we could see them. "Hey, ya'll, we over here." It was something about Bobby that irritated me. I didn't know what, but I was going to make the best of this night.

Anita came over and hugged me. "Hey, girl, I haven't seen you two in a few days. Ain't anybody got to tell me what has been going on it that room. All you had to do was listen at the door." Anita couldn't stop laughing as we gave our tickets to board the ship.

Everybody was dancing, laughing, and talking it seemed, and some people were in the corner just observing and being dignified. Some were wasted and we had not even been off shore for ten minutes. Anita and Bobby were dancing, getting their groove on while holding there drinks in their hand. Melvin asked me what I wanted from the bar.

I told him that I didn't think that I was going to indulge.

"Now look, we only have a couple of days left, let's make the best of it."

I reluctantly told him, "Okay, but just one, Melvin." When he came back, he had a Bahama Mama which was in the largest glass that I had ever seen. "Man, what's that?" I asked.

"Your Bahama Mama is here," he said laughing as he started dancing from side to side, sipping on his drink. "Come on, babe, let's get down with everybody."

Now we were part of the crew on the booze cruise. Anita and Bobby had made their way over to us. "Are you having a good time?" Anita asked.

"Yes, I'm feeling real good on this booze cruise," I yelled. I looked out from the rail upon the blue waters.

Melvin embraced me from behind. "I love you, girl, and I will do anything for you. Don't you ever forget that? It's you and me forever, no matter what."

I looked at the water and begin to feel dizzy. "Melvin, can we go and sit down? I'm not feeling well."

"Okay, babe, hold on."

I opened my eyes with Melvin holding my hand, trying to help wake me up. "Melvin." I couldn't finish my sentence my head was pounding so hard. The boat was finally coming back into port. The music had calmed down and turned mellow. Luckily for me, he put us out directly in front of the hotel. I tip toed back into the lobby. When we all got back upstairs, we all said goodnight to Bobby and Anita. Melvin unlocked the door and I went straight for the bathroom. I should have stuck with my instinct on not drinking on that boat. I came out and plopped right on the bed face down. Melvin came over and undressed me, and told me just relax and try to get some sleep. He gave me a kiss and lay down beside me in the bed. He stroked and caressed my shoulders as I drifted off into a much needed sleep.

The next morning had come and I was awakened by a knock on the door. I looked over and Melvin was not there. I heard the door to our room open. "Thank you, here you go." The door closed and Melvin walked in with a breakfast tray. It had crepes stuffed with cream cheese and strawberries, slices of Canadian bacon, and two fruit cups. "How do you feel?" I sat up finally, not feeling sick as I was the night before.

"Fine, much better. This is so sweet. I love you, baby."

He looked into my eyes. "I love you even more."

The plane was touching back down into reality, we were on our way home. It took one hour from getting off the plane and into our car. All the wonderful things that filled my head from the Island were still there. I reminisced on them the entire time coming home. A text came through my phone I looked and it was Terrance.

Melvin turned to me. "Who is that bothering you already?"

"Oh, it's Sharise wanting to know if we were back yet." Melvin turned back around putting his attention on the street.

We were finally home. Even though we were away, I still missed my home. When we got in, we both sat sown on the sofa. "Man, we have two more days to stay off from work, babe, I guess we can find something fun to do." Melvin started tipping his fingers over to me smiling.

"Oh come on, Melvin, what are you on? Okay, baby, I'm down with that, but for some reason I feel a little tired and my body is feeling a little achy. I guess we had too much fun. Just let me rest a bit. I promise I'll make you happy before we go back to work. I think I'll take a nap to help put me back into reality."

CHAPTER THIRTY TWO

Discovered

I got up from lying around and felt great as I sat up in the bed. I extended my arms out, stretching as I yawned, when suddenly, my eyes caught a glimpse of Melvin's precious chest drawer that he kept locked at all times. I got up and walked over to it. The key was stashed underneath it. I used to laugh about it when Terrance used to tease me about it, but sometimes curiosity gets the better of us. I walked over to it, reached behind it, and grabbed the key to unlock the chest. I was getting ready to unlock it, but another mind told me to leave it alone. Did I want to give him privacy or was I ready to get hurt again like last time I found things that were in his drawer? Our vacation had helped me put that incident in the back of my mind. I remember I was told once that if I went looking for trouble I just might find it, so I left it alone and decided to do something more constructive, like cleaning. I made the front room the last to do. I got to the DVD player and started dusting around. I saw a movie that was still partly in the machine. I thought it was the movie that we had seen the other night, and figured we must have left it out. I figured it was *Obsessed,* the movie with Beyonce' kicking that woman's ass over her husband. I would like to see it again, so I pop it in the DVD player and continued on with my dusting.

I heard moaning sounds of a woman, then, *"Fuck me harder."*

Then, a man's voice, *"Oh yeah, baby, that's it, open wider for me."* It sounded like Melvin. When I turned around, on the T.V. screen I saw Melvin, David, and Lucinda all nude on each other. They were in a porn movie. I popped it out and on the front of it was titled was *Lucinda Does a Double.* It was produced by Fun Productions. I dropped the tape and felt the life draining from my body.

An hour had passed and I was in the same position. I finally felt strength in my body, picked up my purse and keys, and started out the door. I looked back before I left out, and picked up the movie and put it in my purse. I needed to talk to my buddy, so I jumped in my car trying my best to see through all the tears that was clouding up my vision as I was trying to see the street. I tremendously shook as the light turned and the cars behind me blew for me to proceed. I reached down on the dashboard and called Terrance, praying for him to answer.

"Hello."

Thank God he was there. "Terrance, I need to see you."

"What's wrong, Shante? Are you alright? Wait you don't have to tell me, I can sense when something is wrong with my buddy."

"You know, Terrance, that's a shame you know me so well."

"Ah, you know I'm the man. I can feel you through the phone line."

I tried to sound normal as possible and carry a conversation without him detecting the way I was really feeling. "Is your woman over there? "

"Hey now, come on. Ain't you getting a little nosey?" I cracked a smile, but no laughter would come. "Naw, girl, something is wrong I just know it", he said.

I asked him was he busy. "Terrance, can I come over there? I'm so hurt. What I just saw makes me, want to just die."

"Calm down, okay? Are you driving?" I told him that I was. "I need you to stop and pull over and I will come and meet you. Look, where are you now?"

"I'm on New Hampshire Avenue right at the post office on Randolph."

"Okay, pull in the parking lot. I don't want you to drive any further, I really don't like the way you sound."

I pulled into the parking lot and cried uncontrollable. I asked myself about what I felt was going on. I mean, I have had suspicions for a long time, but kept asking myself over and over again, was it just something that was playing tricks on me? Was it the devil pushing me to kill him and I would just lose everything, including my mind? The images kept flashing through my mind. Melvin and Dave were both doing that girl. Ten minutes later, Terrance pulled up. He jumped out of the car and ran over. I jumped out and embraced him so tight, still crying.

"Oh, Terrance, I hate him, I wished he would die."

"Man, he must have done the worst thing to you to hear you

say such harsh words. You have never embraced me so tight like that. What did he do to you?"

"Terrance, I hate him. I don't ever---" Terrence led me to his car. "Come on now, let's get in the car and talk." When we got in the car, Terrance reached into the glove compartment and pulled some tissues out for me. "Now, tell me what happened."

I sobbed and tried to talk through my crying. "Terrance, I feel as though I'm going crazy. Man, sometimes I feel as though it's my own fault. Do you think I'm naive?"

"What makes you feel that way?"

"I don't know, Terrance, I have been feeling like something had been going on right under my nose. You might have told me I was being paranoid, but I found out this morning that my instincts were right."

"What happened so bad to make you feel that way, Shante? Come on now, breathe and talk to me."

"Okay, you know I found that photo and letter a while ago in the drawer? He gave an explanation and I let it go. Then, his whole demeanor as a person, my husband, just seems different to me. He has always has been so loving, and now he has wild ass mood swings if he doesn't know where I am or what I'm doing."

Terrance interrupted me, "Shante, every man acts that way with their woman. What do you expect? You are a gorgeous catch. He is just being territory with you."

"Yeah, that's just it. I'm not a piece of meat, or a human trophy. You know my Ma used to always say, if a nigger act like a jealous fool about you, then he is trying to hide something in his own backyard."

"Come on now, your mama didn't know everything. You know she was from the old school."

"But, Terrance, I didn't say she knew everything, but to me damn near all."

"Okay, calm down."

"Terrance, what about the bizarre behavior he gave me the other night? He felt as though he was going to manhandle me. Not loving at all."

"Hey, he was probably just trying to spice your sex life up. I guess he wanted it another way. You know, the same old way all the time can get pretty boring to some men. I guess he thought you would have liked that."

"Okay, what about secretly talking on the phone in other rooms always with a low tone so I cannot hear him. He either tells me when I ask that he was not on the phone or he was talking to no one."

"Shante, can't you give that man some privacy? A little bit of space. I know you know we all need a little of that now and then."

"You know, Terrance, I'm beginning to wonder whose side you are on. Do you just think I'm talking out the side of my neck? I'm not crazy. Well, we had company the week before we left. It was Melvin's brother, David, and he had brought his friend, Lucinda. We were playing cards and then we watched part of a porn movie that I felt awkward watching with them. Melvin knows that really isn't my thing to do, but I was trying. When they left Lucinda took the movies with her, but I don't know where this shit came from that I found. But obviously it came from all three of them since they were in it fucking each other. That movie was not there when they left."

"Okay what was this movie about, because I know how you can be? If it was a porn movie, I know you are not into that, but you know a lot of guys like to look at those once in a while. And, it's just entertaining and to some a turn on." I looked at him with my tears starting to fall again. I felt it in the corner getting ready to fall. Terrace looked at me. "Look, just don't take any of this the wrong way. It's not anything wrong with a little porn now and then if that's what this is about." "I just told you what it was about, obviously I have to show you"

I asked Terrance to take me over his house. I was still sobbing the entire ride over there. He put his hand on my lap and patted me trying to calm me down. But, little did Terrance know, it was going to take a hell of a lot more to calm me down from this. I just wanted Terrance to know how I had been feeling through all of this, especially after I show him the tape.

We were at his place. Before we got out I looked at him and said, "You know, Terrance, now I know why Ma would sometimes say that one day the scales would fall from my eyes and I would see things for what they really was."

Terrance told me to hold on. He came around and opened the car door for me. He put his arm around me for comfort. He opened his front door and let me in. "Do you want anything?"

"Yeah, do you have any gin?"

"Are you serious? It's a little early to have such a drink."

"Look, Terrance, I know its eleven thirty, but it's almost noon. Please, I need something for my nerves.

He hesitated. "Okay, but only one." He got up and came back with the gin and tonic. I felt it burning my belly as it went straight there, and placed my hand there and held it. I hadn't eaten yet and Terrance sensed that. He went straight to the kitchen and gave me a ham and cheese sandwich that he had in the refrigerator from the day before. I really didn't have an appetite, but he made me eat it anyway. "Now what is this all about Shante?"

I went into my purse and pulled out the movie. I handed it to him. "Put this in and play it. Terrance turned on the DVD and pushed play. While it was coming on with the credits, Terrance was still trying to tell me that Melvin looking at a little porn was a natural thing for a man to do.

"Shante, I can't believe your attitude on things like this. You are the most liberal person with your thoughts on most things and-" Terrance couldn't finish what he was saying, he had lost his words as soon as the movie came on and he saw three nude bodies on the television screen. It wasn't the fact that they were fucking each other silly, it was the fact that Melvin was fucking the girl that he had introduced to me as David's girlfriend. . David was standing over her getting his dick sucked. "He had brought that slut, Lucinda over my house and introduced to me as his fiancé. But we didn't take David serious about that. He had so many girls."

Terrance looked stunned and shocked. The words of comfort and advice had eluded him. He knew at that point it was shit that even he could not explain. Melvin was fucking her just like a porn star, because apparently that was what he was. I was married to a fucking porn star. "What the fuck?" Terrance blurted out. He didn't know what to say. Terrance went into the kitchen poured himself a drink. He brought his glass and the bottle back with him and poured me another.

"Give it to me good, Daddy. I've been such a bad girl."

Her sounds became muffled because David told her to shut up and be a good girl. He shoved his dick back in her mouth. Terrace advanced the tape to another scene. I was so sickened by what I had seen when I had discovered it, but nothing could prepare me for a later scene that Terrance had advanced to. Melvin and his own brother were engaged toward the end of the tape. Lucinda was standing over them in all black leather, holding a whip over them and she was telling Melvin to fuck David real good. I had not seen that, as soon as I did my stomach churned, I felt nauseous, and ran to the bathroom to throw up all that I had just eaten and drank. Terrance had turned the tape off. I heard him swearing under his breath.

"That motherfucking man lover. We both were tripping pretty hard, in fucking disbelief. My cell phone started ringing. Terrence looked at it and asked, "Do you want me to talk to this punk ass mother-"

"No, no, I don't want to talk to him, I just--" I ran over and turned the phone off. My thoughts were scrambled all over again. I hated him and wanted him dead. Terrance came over and embraced me, trying to comfort me again. This was the first time he had no words to soothe me and make me feel better, he just held me and tried to ease my sorrows.

CHAPTER THIRTY THREE

Consultation Is In Order

Four hours had gone by and I awoke on Terrance's sofa. I looked around and he was sitting across from me with his concerned face. "How are you feeling?"

"Hey, I've seen and felt better days." Terrace let out a sigh. He got up and brought me a couple of Tylenol and a glass of water. He knew me so well, even when I didn't feel well. My head was pounding and he just sensed it. I took it from him immediately. "Thanks."

"I was thinking that you could stay here for awhile."

"I know, Terrance, but I have to think very clearly before I do anything. First, I think my first move is to go and get a HIV test and make sure that I am physically okay. Mentally, I can't tell you anything yet. You know I don't think I will be able to ever get those images out of my mind. They are probably going to be in there forever. What kind of life will I ever have? I do know one thing, I want a life, I want a life without Melvin."

Terrance went over to his desk. "You know you need a good lawyer, I can help you with that. My cousin is a lawyer and he owes me one. I know he could help you. " He paused, and then looked at me. "What's wrong, you have a doubtful look on your face, a penny for your thoughts."

I told him where my mind was at the moment. "You know, Terrance, I keep thinking about him and his own brother. What is that about?"

"Man, you and me both. You need some answers about that one. Hell, we both may even a good shrink before it's all over."

Terrance came over to me and started rubbing my back and shoulders. He was trying to get some tension out. But, even he knew that a rub down was only a short fix. My life had been fucked over. He asked me about talking to a lawyer friend before I left. I agreed. Terrence went over to his desk to look for his card. I pulled my phone out and turned it back on. When it came on, Melvin had left twenty five messages.

"Melvin is blowing my phone up."

Terrance shook his head. "You know what, he must know that you are on to him. Don't erase anything, because my cousin is going to need everything to work in your favor if he can help you."

I put my cell phone on speaker as we listened to my messages that I had. *"Shante, give me a call."* Second message, *"Shante where are you? I called about two hours ago. I called your job and they haven't heard from you today. What's going on?"* Third message, *"Okay I know you have lost your damn mind. I know you are skipping work, fucking around somewhere. Don't let me find your ass."* Click. Fourth message, *"Where the fuck are you, Shante? Where the fuck is you? You let me call one more time. It's definitely gonna be me and you."* That one was a trip.

Terrance put his finger up. "Damn, he is really controlling you. Does he think that you are the child he has never had?"

The fifth and six were click hang ups. The seventh he came back. *"Shante, I'm going to kick your ass when I see you. I hope your ass is in the hospital or in jail for your sake."* The eighth and ninth were hang-ups of frustration, I guess. The rest were pretty much the same. The last message was from Greg at work wanting to know where I was. I had to think of something pretty good. I probably had been put on AWOL for the day, but I would have to call Susan and leave a voice message because I knew I would be taking a leave of absence and would be out indefinitely.

Terrance dialed his cousin whose name was Steve Malone. When he reached him, he gave an outline of me and what was going on. When he filled him in on my story, Terrance handed me the phone to talk to him. Steve was in total disbelief. He was interested in taking my case and representing me. He didn't want to get paid until after, he said he was going to win the case. He was very confident. I liked him, so I hired him to represent me. He wanted to meet with me the next day at nine o' clock in the morning.

Terrance insisted that I stayed overnight there, but I told him that I wanted to try and act normal as possible around Melvin. I didn't want him to know that I knew anything was going on. When I left out, Terrence was very nervous for me and I promised him when I got home

I would text him to let him know if I was ok. "Don't worry, everything will be alright. I better go now." I left out to see what was waiting for me.

I drove up and I didn't see Melvin's car, but David's car was there. When I opened the door David was sitting on the couch, alone this time. "Hey, baby doll, what's up?"

The images filled my head of him in that movie, but I tried to get past that and act normal. "Oh nothing, I'm just kickin' it."

"Melvin went to pick up some chicken from Popeye's."

"Oh, do you need anything?" I asked.

"No, I can get it. I know you must be tired just getting home from work."

"No, I took the day off and spent it with my sister, Sharise. She really was not feeling well today. I think she has got food poisoning, so I went with her to the hospital. We were there practically the whole day. My cell phone was turned off, so I couldn't receive or call out on my cell phone. It was all so hectic. Anyway, she is feeling a little better now."

"Oh, you know Melvin was raging when he couldn't get in touch with you. I was here trying to calm him down." David got up and walked out the door because he heard Melvin's music from his car coming in the driveway. They were talking, and then shortly after that they came in. Melvin temper was gone. "Hey, babe, David told me about Sharise. Is she okay? Man, where had she eaten last?"

"I'm not sure, but she was in pretty bad shape. She finally got treated."

"That's good," Melvin said. David came around and grabbed a chicken breast out of the box. Melvin came over and tried to kiss me in my mouth. I turned and his lips hit my cheek. "Hey, what was that?" he asked.

"Huh, what did you say?" I was acting real dumbfounded. I never wanted his lips to ever touch me again. "You know, baby, I'm so tired from today's events, I need to just go to sleep. I am dead tired." He told me okay and I retired to the bed. I closed the door, then got my cell phone and called Terrence and let it ring once to let him know everything was okay.

A couple of hours had passed and Melvin came into the room quietly. I never moved a muscle. I didn't want him to try anything. He turned off the lights and got into the bed, cuddling up behind me on my back. I could feel his manhood touching me, fully erect, but I never moved a muscle. He started calling my name. "Shante. Shante, wake up, baby." If it wasn't for my heart beating, he could have pronounced me dead. I felt sick inside and my skin was started to crawl just form knowing his body was touching me. He finally gave up and turned away to the other corner of the bed.

Saturday morning was different because Melvin was actually in the bed. He was usually gone, traveling for his job. But, I knew better now. He was involved in porno flicks. I guess everyone needed a rest. I crept slowly out of the bed, careful not to wake him. When I got on my feet, he stirred in the bed and I froze as though I was trying to get away with stealing something. He never opened his eyes. He settled back down and he started to lightly snore. I gathered up a pair of jeans and a top. I tip toed into the bathroom, closed the door, and quietly washed up. I preferred the shower, but I knew the water would wake him. That would lead him into wanting a shower fuck, and as long as I could help it I didn't want that to ever happen again.

I left a note on the table telling Melvin that I had to go run a few errands. I left out and was off to see my lawyer. As I drove down Wisconsin Avenue, my thoughts were what my next move would be. I arrived right on time. I was dead set on leaving Melvin, but I have to have the timing right. I would have to wait for him to go on one of his famous business trips to make my move. I needed to find a place to go. I had saved some money up and I had to find a place where he couldn't track me. My mind was on so much as I knocked on Steve Malone's door. He came to the door with a great big smile as he greeted me.

He extended a hand shake out to me. "Mrs. Brenin. Very nice to meet you, you can just call me Steve."

"Hello, Steve, nice to meet you." He had a nice office with beautiful cherry wood furniture and suede to compliment it. "Nice office."

"Thanks, I try my best. Sit down, Mrs. Brenin, and talk to me about your problem. My cousin has told me that you are good people. I know that sounds like a shrink asking you to spill your guts, but in my line of work, I like to know where you are coming from and analyze that with what I can help you with." Steve made me feel so comfortable with him that I told him everything. He went over to his small refrigerator cooler in the corner and asked me did I want some bottled Perrier water. "Yes, please."

He opened the bottle and sat down, looking like he was in disbelief. "Wow, I would have pulled out a beer, but that would not be professional at all. Mrs. Brenin, do you want to stay with your husband?"

"Hell to the no. Excuse my French, but I hate him. And my Ma and Da never raised me to hate, but they didn't teach me anything about what I have been through. I never thought anything like this even existed. You know, Steve, I feel like I am a sponge. I have taken so much shit all of my life. A lot of times I never say anything, do anything. Well, I want that to stop now. I just can't absorb anymore." My cell phone started ringing. I looked at it and it was Melvin. I put my finger up to my lips, motioning Steve not to say anything. "Hello. Oh, hey, baby, I see you're up already. I know, baby, but I had to run some errands for Sharise. I'll be home soon. Okay, I love you, too. Bye, see you soon."

Steve looked at me and said, "I can see that you are you scared of him, Shante."

"Not so much scared, but frightened."

"There is not so much difference in the two. They sort of go hand in hand. From that conversation, he doesn't know that you know anything about his other lifestyle?"

"No, he doesn't know that I know what he is doing on the side. But, I don't know how much longer I can go on with this charade of acting normal, like everything is peaches and cream with us."

"Well, do you want me to get some papers served on him?"

"Since he goes out of town so much, I was going to wait and pack my stuff and just leave. Do you think that's a good idea? And then, get some papers served on him then for divorce."

"You just tell me when you're ready. In the meantime, try and get all the evidence you can against him. We would definitely need that in the hearing. Do you have the tape with you?" I nodded my head, went in my bag, took it out, and handed it to him. "Try and not let him know that you're on to him, because you are still in the house. If he knew he would get rid of all the evidence you would need at the hearing."

"Well, I better get back." We stood up and shook hands again then said our goodbyes. As I walked away he called out to me.

"Mrs. Brenin, be safe."

I was on my way when I remembered that I was supposed to have gone to see my sister and run some small errands. I knew Melvin would want to know everything, so I called Sharise and had a chat because I didn't have time to actually visit her. I told her everything about my trip and I asked her how things were going at home. She said that Vance was doing a little better. I didn't want to tell her about my troubles, so we talked in general. We told each other that we love one another, and then hung up. I passed by a drugstore and went in, and picked up some items that I needed at home. I was a block away from home when I pulled over and dialed my buddy. "Hey, what's up, Terrance?"

"You tell me. Are your alright?"

"Yeah, things are going smooth so far."

"What has your crazy ass man been doing?"

"He tried some dumb shit last night, but he will never touch these goodies again."

"I just don't know how you are going to pull this off. Eventually, you are going to act all the way normal or tell him. I mean, he is going to want a normalcy from you and that means fucking or sucking or something. When you turn all the way cold turkey, he is going to suspect something. When are you planning to leave?"

"I don't know, Terrance. As soon as he has his next business trip, I am going to jet out on his dodge."

"Do you even know where you are going to go?"

"No, it's too much to even think about, but I've got to do this right now."

"Why don't you come and stay with me?"

"That's sweet; Terrance, but I would never endanger you like that. I better go, I'll try and call you later. Bye." We hung up and I was on my way home.

CHAPTER THIRTY FOUR

Still Trying To Feel Me Out

I spotted Melvin looking out the window as I drove up the driveway. He came out the door and met me. Thank God I decided to stop to the store so I had bags to prove that I was there. "Shante, why didn't you wake me? You know I would've gone to the store with you."

"Melvin, I know that you were tired, and besides, it was just a few things that I needed, it's cool." We went in the house. Melvin was playfully pulling on me. When I put the bags down he got behind me and stared humping me. "Come on, Melvin. I thought I gave you plenty on the Islands."

"Baby, come on, I got a big appetite."

The flashes presented themselves in my mind again of Melvin, that girl, and his own brother doing unimaginable things with each other. I quickly turned around and told him that I wanted to start cooking. "I wanted to try a new recipe. I've been dying to try this dish. And as for you, it's not like I don't want to do it. I thought I pleased you so much on the vacation, well, baby, I need a break."

He looked at me and said, "Damn, girl, I thought you would want more. In fact, I want you and need you right now. What is the problem?"

I sighed. "Baby, there is no problem. I'll make it up to you just let me start my dinner. You satisfied me so much, I am so fulfilled. I guess you're too much man sometimes for me."

"But it will soon, like tonight?"

"Maybe." Melvin left and told me he was going to see how David was doing. "Okay, I'll see you when you get back."

When he left out, I let a sigh of relief. I didn't know how I was going to keep this up. I went into the bedroom and started snooping. I had to find out more dirt on him. I went straight to his chest and ran my hand underneath for the key. I never felt it. He had moved it. I got a flashlight and looked under the case. It had been moved. I looked for the photo and the letter of that girl, and that, too, was gone. He was trying to clean up behind himself. I looked inside his dresser under his clothes. He had no trace of anything. I went to the kitchen, wondering what was up. I started dinner and thought of what my next move should be. The phone rang and it was Melvin.

"Hey, baby, I'm over at David's house. He wanted me to ask you did you happen to see his movie that he left over the other night."

I heard David in the background. "Hey, Shante."

"He said it was a rental, and he has to return it or either pay for it if it got lost."

I was about to expose the both of them. I guess they knew that the tape was missing and didn't know how to get around asking me about it. That was probably why Melvin had been acting so strange lately. I remembered what my lawyer had told me, 'Be cool,' so I told him no.

"Hey, you ready to eat? Dinner is almost ready."

"Girl, what the hell, do you have an attitude about something?"

"No. I'll see you when you get home."

Melvin had me where he wanted me, at home, and he was still in the touching mood. He came up to me while I was placing the food on the table. "Come on, baby, give me dessert before dinner, like you usually do."

I squirmed from him. "Come on, Melvin, I don't want your surprise to get cold." I led him to the table where I had prepared his favorite, a rack of lamb, mashed potatoes with pearled onions, and slightly blanched green beans with sliced almonds.

His face lit up. "Baby, when did you find time to do all of this?"

"Just sit." I brought out some nice red wine that we have been saving for a special moment. The special moment that I had in mind was different in thought from his. I was sure.

"Baby, what are we celebrating tonight?" I held up my glass to him. "Oh, baby, just happy that the two of us are still together?"

He held his up. "Yeah, that's what's up. And, I hope tonight it's on also."

Man there he goes again. I knew I had better think of something soon, because the night was young. We had finished dinner and Melvin told me how tasty the food was. He went into the family room to watch television while I was in the kitchen cleaning up. When I finished, I came up behind the chair.

"Hey, baby, I'm really tired, so I'm going to go to bed now, O.K."

"What? It's early. Don't even try it. I'll be right behind you."

Man, he would not give up. I went in the bathroom, and locked the door. *Think, think, I don't have much time. I'm finding myself in this bathroom more often trying to think of ways not to engage in letting Melvin fuck me anymore.* I looked in the mirror. "Come on, Shante, think."

Melvin turned the knob and found that it was locked. "Shante, girl, what are you doing in there, are you coming?"

"Yeah, I'll be right there." I turned on the water, put my hands under, lifted some water up to my face, and splashed it. I took a towel to dry my face. *Man, I didn't want Melvin to ever touch me again.*

"Shante, come on, baby, I'm waiting."

I looked down at my magazine rack and looked at a page that was flipped. There was an ad about yeast infections. I looked in my medicine cabinet and saw a tube of Monistat cream. I filled the tube and inserted it. When I came out I went to Melvin and sat down beside him on the edge of the bed. "Baby, I know I have been acting strange, but I thought by now my situation would be better."

Melvin looked at me strangely. "What are you talking about, Shante? What situation?" He kept pawning at my blouse.

I grabbed his hand. "Look, Melvin, I didn't want to tell you, but I've got a bad yeast infection. I just can't do anything with you right now."

"What? Where did you get that come from?"

"I don't know. It just happens sometimes. You are going to have to be patient."

"Well, okay, but you should have just told me. I would not have been thinking on it so hard.

I rolled my eyes. "Look, I'm not in the mood for anything right now, okay? It's not anything personal."

"Okay, babe, I was just kidding, I can wait."

I knew I had to calm down. "Look, when you think that you will have to travel for your job again?"

"Well, it may be about two weeks, not unless I'm called in to go somewhere. Why?"

"Oh, I was just asking. I wanted to be able to send my baby off the right way that's all." I kissed his cheek. "Good night, Melvin."

"Goodnight, Shante."

I laid on my pillow thinking, *You no good motherfucker, those two weeks can't come fast enough.*

CHAPTER THIRTY FIVE

The Truth Can Hurt Sometimes

Finally, I was back to work sitting at my desk, looking at all the task I had to do that was left for me in the two week period that I was gone. Funny, it was just two weeks ago I couldn't wait to leave here and relax. Now, it feels almost like a retreat, some solitude, a piece of mind, a place to hide in even. I started reading through my menus on the computer. Susan had fired a lot of people that had been there from the beginning. I knew she was working on me, but I knew I couldn't let that happen, especially now that I would be supporting myself soon. Susan was changing so many things that Mr. Harris had worked so hard for. His policies were half done away with and she seemed to fill the office with acquaintances of hers. They would try to mingle in with us and act as though they barely knew her, but I saw right through their acts. It seemed the only one that played in her hands was stupid ass Greg. I wondered if he was ever going to wake up and smell the coffee. A lot of my co workers came in to welcome me back, asking me how I enjoyed the Cayman Islands. I talked with them while still trying to work.

It was about lunch time when Susan came in without any greeting or anything, and she had not seen me in two weeks. She just started with her demands of what she wanted done. I just looked at her and in the middle of what she was saying cut her off. "Hello, Susan, how are you doing today?"

She stopped talking as though I was speaking a foreign language to her. "What?"

"It's called greeting someone, especially when you haven't seen that person for awhile. It's common courtesy."

She was stunned that I had even gone there. She stumbled over her words. "Well, hey."

Damn, where did her people skills come from? And how did she get this job? She started talking again, still without saying good morning. She told me for a meeting that afternoon she had to present some numbers that Greg had already went over and gave the okay on them. All I needed for you to do was put them in a form that she could present to the board. "Okay, sure, Susan, I'll have them for you by three."

"No, I want them by one."

"Look, Susan, it's my first day back from vacation. I've been working all morning very hard. I have not taken a break or my lunch. But, I am getting ready to take my lunch. We do have some union rules that we go by. If you would pull out the union rules and look at number four dash three, it states that every employee has one hour lunch during an eight hour day, so what's it going to be, I take my lunch or I call head quarters to ask them to help you through understanding the rules that we had had in place for many years now."

She left out. "That's fine, bitc-." I didn't quite hear the last bit of that word she mumbled as she walked out. I knew what she wanted to say, but that was just fine. I would be the number one bitch in that office if I had to.

I called Terrance and asked about lunch. "What's up, Shorty?"

"Let's get some lunch."

"We can do that. I'll see you then." Sometimes he tried to be so hip.

At the usual place, the Bistro, Terrance and I enjoyed two wonderful Cobb salads with my nice glass of White Zinfandel, and he had his Heineken beer. "I'm really worried about you, Shante. I mean, I hope he doesn't suspect that..."

I held up my hand before he could even finish what he was saying. "Suspect, why are we having this conversation about him suspecting me? What about a conversation about what the fuck he has done to me. I've been living with a nigger on the down low, and can't even tell you for how long my guess is as go as yours."

"Hey, I was just saying that does he suspect that you are on to him."

"You know, honestly, I think he knows. Why all of a sudden his shit is moved out from my sight in the bedroom. And all of this after I found that tape. He probably is terrified about me finding it. And, now he is trying to fuck me every minute of the day. My rejections have probably got him wondering."

Terrance was shaking his head. "Yeah, you're right, he probably knows that something is going on in that head of yours. Man, I really will feel so much better when you are able to leave."

"I know you and me both."

Back at the office, my cell phone rang. I opened my purse and pressed the talk button after I looked at the ID and saw that it was Steve, my lawyer. "Hello, Shante, how are you doing?"

"Oh, hello, Steve, I'm doing fine considering."

"Well, that's good. Are you able to talk right now?"

"Yes, hold on." I got up to close the door then returned to talk.

"We need to talk about your case. I had a staff member to look up some interesting finds about your husband. Are you sure that you are sitting down?"

"Yes."

"Okay, Mr. David Brenin, your husband's brother, well he is not your husband's blood brother, which explains him being in the video. Let me rephrase that, nothing explains that shit for anybody, but he is not his blood brother. His name is David Ely Smith. However, they went to college together and are frat brothers. So, we can put that in our file."

I just stared into space in disbelief. All of those years, I thought that they were really brothers. That explained a lot from when I first met him at his mom's house, with the coldness he had when we first met. And the argument, I started wondering was it about me? Then, I thought about him being at our house all the time. I felt like a first class ass and fool because everything was right under my nose.

"Shante? Shante?" There was complete silence. I couldn't believe what I was hearing. I felt like I was in a dream. "Shante, are you okay?"

"No, Steve, I'm not, I--." He interrupted the little words that were trying to come out of my mouth.

"I understand if you want me to call you back."

"No, Steve, we can continue talking. "

"Okay, now the bank account that you told me about. His income was being made by another career that he has chosen."

"What do mean another career? He delivers supplies in

different cities."

"The first job you told me about was the regional supplier, he left that company a while ago, about a year and a half now. He has a new career and it's in the porn industry. Melvin is a porn star with Fun Productions. David is doing the same kind of work, as well as the female who was in that particular film. I know you are concerned about your health, especially now, but, Shante, I advise that you consider regular HIV testing because of his activities. Stuff like this really shakes me up. I know that you are a good woman. What bothers me is the way some men mess over the good ones like you." I bit down on my lip as a tear rolled down my face. "Well, do you still want to pursue this?"

"Yeah, I hope that he has to travel soon because I need to leave as soon as I can. I will call you in a few days."

"Okay, thank you, Bye."

The clock was ticking and I had to set my mind on getting the report ready. It was a good thing she told me not to touch the numbers or change anything. As soon as I looked at the numbers, I saw several mistakes from just a slight glance. But, like I said, Susan made very specific about not changing anything. This was one time I that I was really glad to follow her orders. This time, I was going to let her sink. I finished putting them on a new spread sheet. I placed them in an envelope and put them on the letter holder outside Susan's door. I went back to my office, closed the door, and cried for the hurt that I was feeling, and praying that my health would endure well and that I had not contracted HIV. My cell phone was ringing. I looked and it was Melvin. I let it ring. I couldn't even pretend to talk in a normal manner. Shortly after, my desk phone was ringing. I looked at it and it was still Melvin. Why was he still acting as though he wanted to be bothered by me? When I didn't answer, my cell was being rung again. That time, he left a message. I listened to it.

"Shante, why aren't you picking up your phone? When you get this, call me back." I wanted to take off, but I had to think about the leave I would need when the time came for me to make my move. Melvin was ringing my cell phone again.

That time I answered it. "Hello."

"Shante, I've been trying to reach you. Where are you?"

"I'm here at work."

"You must have just got there because I've been calling." I was rubbing my forehead because he was irritated me with his interrogation questioning.

"Look, Melvin, what do you want? I really wish you would stop asking me all of these fucking questions. Right now, I don't have time."

"Who in the fuck do you think you are talking to like that?"

"I think I am fucking talking to you. Stop acting as though I am your child and you are my father. Look, I got to go." I hung up. He started blowing my phone up again. This time, I ignored it and was on my way home.

CHAPTER THIRTY SIX

Trouble Don't Last Always

When I pulled up into the driveway, Melvin was at home. It was one day I wished my driveway would be empty. When I walked in he was waiting for me. He rushed up to me and slapped me. The stinging brought tears to my eyes. I dropped my purse and held the side of my face. "Shante, you make me so mad. What was all of that shit about today when we were talking on the phone? What has gotten into you? Don't you know that I love you? What is wrong with you?"

I ran into the bathroom crying. I lay down on the bed holding the side of my face. I couldn't believe that he hit me. He had never laid a hand on me all the years we had been together. I felt that I could kill him if I had the nerve, but that was not in my nature.

I stayed in my bed in a fetus position for an hour. I heard Melvin on the phone talking to someone about a job that he had to go to. I hoped that it was going to be my final moments to put my thoughts about leaving him come true. He finally came in the bedroom and sat on the bed.

"Shante, I'm really sorry about what happened earlier. There was no excuse for me to put my hands on you, I'm sorry, baby. Will you forgive me?"

"It's okay, maybe I shouldn't have been so rude to you on the phone earlier. I'm sorry, too." He reached down to try and kiss me on my lips, but I turned away just in time for him to kiss the side of my face. Melvin told me that he had a job in Nevada. That was the sweetest thing that Melvin had said to me in awhile. How long I'd waited to hear that. He was finally giving me a queue to do my thing and leave his ass. "Oh, baby, when do you have to leave?"

"Well, I know you hate short notices, but I'll have to leave early in the morning. I would have told you sooner, but I just got the call last night. I didn't want to wake you, so that's why I'm just telling you."

"Well, for how long this time?"

"It will about two weeks again. You know, I was hoping that I could get some of my pussy before I left, what do you say?"

"Melvin, I wish I could, but I'm still not feeling well. I made and appointment to see what's going on with me."

"Good, because I haven't been able to get any since that trip we took and it's almost a month now. My nuts is about to burst." He put his hands on my shoulder. "Are you sure, baby, what about that luscious mouth of yours?"

Is he kidding? I thought to myself. Melvin always hinted around about blow jobs, but little did he know that would never happen in this lifetime again. I was thinking he didn't know how bad I just wanted him to not exist. "No, honey, I'm just not in the mood."

"You know, baby, they have Viagra now for women. Why don't you ask your doctor about it on your next visit?"

I know he had lost his damn mind. I tried to act shocked about this news. "Really, I didn't know that."

"No, really, they make those for women." If only he could read my mind. It didn't matter because I didn't want him. "Never heard of that."

CHAPTER THIRTY SEVEN

Time To Make My Move

The next morning when I opened my eyes, Melvin had left. He left a rose on his pillow beside me, like he used to a long time ago. I sat up looked at the rose and sighed. "Well, brother, it's a bit too late for that." I picked up the phone and called the office, and told them that I had an emergency and would have to go on emergency leave of absence. I hung up, then got washed up and dress. I called Terrance and asked if he wouldn't mind helping me move my shit out. "Oh yeah, can you picked up some boxes?"

He was more than happy to help. "I'll be there in an hour."

I picked up the phone and called my lawyer. "Hey, Steve, today is the day that you can file those papers."

"Alright, I'm on it."

I started folding my clothes and gathering things that were dear to me. I looked up across the room and that chest caught my eye. I went to it and tried to open it, and it was locked as it always was. I looked for the key and still didn't see it. I reached and grabbed a hairpin and tried to pick the lock, and the lock just wouldn't give. *What am I doing?* I thought. "To hell with it." When I withdrew the pin, the lock clicked and gave. I opened it and looked in, and I was taken back in disbelief from what I saw. There were photos of myself, Anita, and Bobby, the couple we had met on the ship. We were all engaged in sexual acts. I shook uncontrollably. My ability at the moment to think was lost. The doorbell rang. I ran to it and Terrance dropped the boxes he was carrying.

"Shante, are you alright? What's wrong? Are you alright?" "I was crying at the same time as I was explaining to him. I held the photo up to him. "What the fuck is that?" Wait." Terrance dragged the boxes in the door and closed it. "Shante, calm down. Calm down, please. Damn, I hate to see you like this."

I calmed down and pulled him in the bedroom. "Terrance, that motherfucker had to have drugged me on that booze cruise we took in the Cayman Islands. I don't remember any of this. I was so curious about that chest. I just had to see what was else was in it. I picked the lock because he always locks it and put the key away. While packing, my curiosity got the better of me. I just had to see. When I got in this is what I found." Terrance looked in and pulled out a letter. It was addressed to me. He started reading it.

Dear Shante,

Even though this is my private area, I know you too well. You are a smart girl with an intuition that even a pad lock couldn't keep you away from. You see, Shante, I admit I was wrong to not tell you from the beginning about things in my life, but when I met you, I fell in love with you. All of the other stuff that I deal with is not real, but you are and I care about you. The day you found that tape I knew it. You went on and pretended not to know about it, but I knew better, you are too smart for the pretense. And I know you have found out about David not being my real brother. It was him who left that tape behind because we had been lovers for awhile, but my heart has been gone from him when you came into my life. I love you and that's all that matters. I'm sorry David left that tape out intentionally for you to find to hurt you. I've already dealt with him about that. It has already been taken care of. But I couldn't lose you, that's why I did drug you on that ship and believe it or not, we made a movie that is an interest of my boss at the studio. But I did not sign the release form because I'm leaving that on you. It all depends on you. But I didn't do it to hurt you, I did it because I love you and now we share something very special between the two of us.

Love Melvin

P.S. Don't ever think about leaving me because I told you we were forever always

Terrance was stunned. "He is a sick motherfucker, damn." Terrence looked more into the chest. There was a copy of the tape entitled *Booze Cruise Booty*. I didn't want to see the tape. There were also pictures they had staged with everybody engaged.

Terrance helped me finish packing. We packed Terrance's truck and put the rest in my car. I went back into the house and gave my last look. That chest was still in my view. "You got everything, Shante?"

"Well, there is one last thing. Come help me with it." I went into the bedroom and grabbed one end of the chest. "Grab that end and help me out to the back yard."

"You mean you want to take this, too? This is not going to fit. The truck is already packed."

"This won't be going in the truck. In fact, it won't be going very far, just in the back." We took in the back near the barbeque pit and sat it down. I grabbed the lighter fluid and started putting fluid all over it.

"No you not. Are you really?" Before Terrance could say another word, I lit a match and threw it in Melvin's precious chest. The chest of secrets was in flames. Terrance reached in quickly and took out the tape and a couple of those pictures. "You never know, you might need this for evidence." Everything was burning and going up in smoke, but I was sure he had a master copy somewhere. We waiting for ten minutes, then Terrance turned on the water hose and put the rest of the flames out. I looked around for my last look, and then I turned around and looked forward because that's where I was headed.

I drove to a storage facility in Fairfax, Virginia and arranged to rent a small unit for fifty nine ninety nine a month. I paid for the unit and bought a lock and some extra keys. I came outside where Terrence helped me unload the cars. We neatly stacked the boxes and placed the padlock on. I asked Terrence about the tape and pictures.

"I think that I'll drop that off to Steve's office for you."

"Okay, that will be fine." I got into my car and my thoughts were frozen.

Terrance walked over to the passenger side. "Shante, let me in on the other side." I opened the door and he got in. "A penny for your thoughts. What's up, what are you thinking about right now?"

"You know, Terrance, I've been doing a lot of thinking on the way over here and basically I am fucked, Melvin has fucked me real good. He is blackmailing me, threatening me with that sex movie he made with me in it. He has already said that we should be in the marriage together forever. I can't stay here. I think I'm going to have to leave."

"And go where, Shante?"

"I was really thinking on the terms of the Virgin Islands. I wasn't playing when I said it before. That's where I'm planning to go."

"You know that could cost a fortune. Have you saved up that much?"

"Hell no, but Melvin has. I'm going to go and withdraw his money right out and leave. Fuck him, that's what I'll do."

"Are you sure? Is your name on his account? Couldn't he have you arrested?"

"No, Terrance, I'm tired of being scared to say or do anything, but today, I think I've made up my mind to do this."

"Are you sure? You have to plan carefully. Right now, I think you are acting on your emotions."

"Hell no, did he plan carefully when he goes off and fuck everybody and anybody he wants? I'm tired of this shit. I want to be satisfied and happy, and I think that this is what it's going to take."

"Well, did you talk to Steve about this?"

"I don't know what he will say. I am going to call him and ask his opinion."

"Why don't you do that now?"

I took my cell phone and speed dialed Steve's number. "Hello, Steve Malone attorney at law."

"Hey, Steve, what's going on?"

"Hey, Shante, how have you been doing?"

"I wanted to ask your opinion on something."

"Okay, shoot."

"Things have changed drastically with my situation."

"I hope for the better."

"No, unfortunately not. Well one good thing, today was the day that Melvin left for another one of his famous business."

"Oh yeah, where to this time?"

"Well he said Nevada, Las Vegas."

"Damn, that's a good one. Doesn't he know that's a real odd place to say that you are going to?"

"This morning when I started packing, I go and started snooping around. When I do, I find sexually explicit pictures of me and a couple that we met on our vacation. A movie was also made with all of them and me. But, I don't remember any of it. I know someone had to have drugged me. And I felt like Melvin knew I would find it. It seems like he wants to blackmail me."

"Do you remember the names of the couple?"

"Yeah, their names were Bobby and Anita. I don't think they mentioned a last name. He says he loves me and that he never wants us to part, no matter what."

"I can't believe what I'm hearing. Normally, I would never do what I'm thinking about doing, but Terrance is my cousin and he really talks highly of you. He is really worried about you so I can believe that I am going to do this but in all the years that I have been practicing law I've never heard of anything like this. You know I want to help you. I am going to put my ethics aside and I'm going to help you as a friend. With all the ammunition that he has, I know you don't want him to use them against you, so we got to get him and stick him with what will hurt worst, and that's his pockets. His account has your name on it, doesn't it?"

"I don't know, but when he told me to withdraw some money that day, it didn't seem to be a problem."

"Okay, then he must have you and authorized user to use the account. Good, check the balance. I heard you said that you said that you want a new start and that probably can be arranged. This is against everything that I believe in, but I'm going to help you out. I'm going to run a check on that couple that you met on the cruise. It sounds to me that they were in on this little plot of Melvin's. He probably knew them. That hook up was too damn easy, excuse my French. But this shit has made me mad as hell. You are too good of a woman to fuck over like this. Anyway, I am going to call you back in two days. Don't do anything until then. Try not to even be in contact with anyone. Think hard and have a plan for where you want to go. And, don't let anyone know where you are and that might include your family. That includes your sister not unless you are one hundred percent sure that you can trust her."

"What about the divorce papers? Are you still going to send them?"

"Yeah, that will throw him off track, and give him the impression that I know nothing about your whereabouts when I represent you in court. I'll tell the judge that I am representing you on the evidence we have against him. I will need the letter you said that he wrote. He is smart and then not so smart, because that letter he wrote is sort of a confession. To cause you no embarrassment of that tape being shown, I will not have you in the chambers with it. If I plan my time right, you will be in the Virgin Islands like you always wanted with all expenses paid courtesy of Mr. Melvin Brenin."

"You mean that we are going to clean him out?"

"We can leave him a little to live on, but I want to set up you account up so it will be making interest for many years to come."

"That would make me feel good if it could really be pulled off. What about the bank, I know they will not release and close that account."

"Come on, Shante, I'll handle it, okay. Just trust me. And if there is a problem about the bank, I'll handle that also. I'll call you back in two days on Terrance's cell number because your cell phone can probably be traced. Turn it off now and get rid of it."

"Okay, I will." We hung up. Terrance looked at me with so much concern.

"Well what now?" I filled him in and told him everything Steve told me.

"I better call Sharise and see how things are going."

Terrance gave me his cell and I dialed the number. It rang and she answered. "Hello."

"Sharise, girl, how are you?" Sharise was quiet and I knew that was a bad sign.

"I'm doing okay."

"And how are my nieces and nephews?"

"They are doing well."

"What about Vance?"

"He is about as well as he can be."

"What do you mean, Sharise?"

"Shante, I stared at him last night after he got in. He was exhausted from wherever he came from. I'm not stupid, I know he was with some bitch last night. I could smell liquor on his breath; he had the smell of sex ranking from his body. If he wasn't so drunk, I know he would have made it to the shower and washed the stench of the bitch he was with. I got up and looked in his jacket pocket and tool out his unopened rubbers there. I can't take anymore. I want him out of the picture, but he won't leave. Shante, I am so sorry for messing this up. Ma and Da worked hard for us to have a nice, comfortable life. They looked after us even after death, so to speak. And I just fucked it all up." Sharise started crying.

"Calm down, Sharise." It wasn't long that I joined in and shed tears with her. When we both calmed down, I thought of a great idea. "Wouldn't it be good if we sold the family house and bank the money and could get a new start somewhere like Atlanta, Georgia?"

"Whoa, that would be a dream comes true."

"Is Vance home?"

"No, why?"

"I love you, Sharise, and we are the only ones left, and your sweet babies, my nieces and nephews. I feel that we could have a better life, I know how, but the sacrifice that you are going to have to make is leaving Vance. We should put the house up on the market and sale it. I have a friend who can handle everything."

"What are you talking about? What about Melvin?"

"Sharise, there are some things I haven't told you because I knew you were going through it. I didn't want to worry you with my problems. For awhile, Melvin and I have not been doing so well."

"What do you mean? Didn't the two of you just come back from a romantic getaway from the Cayman Islands?"

"Yes, but I have had my suspicions about Melvin for awhile."

"What do you mean, Shante? I thought he was the perfect husband. He got you whatever you wanted. You seem so happy, at least that what you used to always tell me. I thought you and Melvin had it all together."

"At one time we did. I loved him with all my heart, but things changed drastically."

"What do you mean? I mean, what did he do that was so awful that you can't patch up and make work? Look at all the times that Vance and I have been together."

"Look, Sharise, you and Vance are in no way comparable with Melvin and I. I used to think that we had the perfect marriage. Nothing could disturb what we had, but I was wrong, so wrong. At first I felt that something wasn't quite right, and then I started dismissing little things. I never confronted him, which was a mistake. I let too much go by."

"I still don't understand, Shante, tell me what happened."

"You know for years I thought Melvin was a regional supply manager. I knew he had to travel. He used to even deliver on my job. Well, one day he told me, oh yeah your office is not on my list anymore. We had to cut extra expenses and your deliveries were on my list to cut.

It didn't even faze him. I always thought that delivering to my office was special to him. We had made such good memories that we made there."

"Come on, Shante, you know men don't cherish things the way we do. We could give them a wonderful pleasure and they feel good at the moment, but when it's time for them to go they are gone until the next time they want some more ass."

"That's harsh, Sharise, but I guess it as some truth to it."

"It's that what this mess is all about?"

"Hell no, let me tell you the rest. Well he started traveling more than usual on his so call business trips."

"Oh my God, does he have some kids, and another family somewhere?"

"No, Sharise, just let me tell you the rest of the story. I found out he was not even working for the supply company anymore. He had a job alright but it wasn't with supplies."

Sharise couldn't help but to interrupt. "Where the hell was he working?"

"Melvin, your brother in law, is working in porno productions. He is one of the casting actors."

"Wha-- What in the hell did you say? You mean to tell me that Melvin is fucking for a living? Oh my God, I can't believe it."

"It's true, Sharise, that's why I have left him. I'm on my friend's phone right now. Mine is off and you won't be able to call that number again."

"Well can I call this phone back? It didn't have and ID showing when I picked it up."

"My friend is very private and doesn't want his name and number out there."

"Shante, where is Melvin right now? I mean, does he know where you are?"

"No."

"Shante, all of this is really hard to believe. How do you even know that this is true? I mean, did somebody tell you all of this shit about Melvin?"

"It's true, Sharise. He had the nerve to have left a copy of one of his movies at the house. But, you have to hear the rest. You know David?"

"Yeah, what about him?"

"That's not even his brother."

"What?"

"Yeah, he has lied to me the entire time of our marriage. To make it worst he and David were in this movie with a skank that had been over my house talking about she was David's girlfriend, and turns out he and David was in the same movie doing her and each other. I really started hating him after that."

"Oh, Shante, I'm so sorry. That motherfucking dog. Where are you now?"

"Sharise, I first want to ask you something? How are feeling about what I asked you earlier, about leaving and putting the house up for sale?"

Shante's response was delayed. "What do you mean? I mean I can't just up and leave. I mean, Vance is, and well he is not as bad as what you as what you just told me about Melvin. I mean, I know he has his moments, but always seem to snap back, you know. I don't think that there are any relationships that are smooth as a baby bottom. I mean, you know what I mean, Shante?"

I knew from her response that I would not be talking to my sister after that night. I just couldn't risk letting Melvin find me or know where I was going to. I knew that she would be the first place that Melvin would go around to find me. I wanted her and the kids to come with me so we could start fresh. It was killing me. I didn't want to abandon her, but I had no choice. "Well, don't worry about it. I am wishing you and Vance the best."

"Why you say it like that? You sound like you are going on another trip on somewhere."

"Girl, you are crazy. Let me speak to those sweet babies." She called them to the phone one by one. I talked to them and told them that auntie Shante loved them and would see them later.

Sharise got back on the phone, "Now, girl, let's go out for lunch again so we can talk this shit over."

"Okay, I'll call you about it later."

"Okay, bye, love you, sis."

I hung up with heaviness in my heart. I loved her and wanted to tell her so much what my plans were going to be, but I couldn't. I started crying and Terrance came over to me.

"Hey, it's going to be alright." We were still standing in the storage unit. Terrance embraced me so tight. It made felt really good and safe. His body was rock solid. He gently lifted my face up by placing his fingers under my chin. He wiped the tears that fell from my eyes and shushed me to stop crying. "Come on now, Shante, you know how I hate to see you cry. I think it hurts me more than it's hurting you when you cry." I managed to put a small smile on my face. "That's it. You know I feel everything is going to be alright, you'll see. Hey, will you please stay over at my house tonight? I promise I won't bite." Terrance always managed to make me smile.

I finally agreed. "Okay, let's go." We locked the unit and I followed him home.

CHAPTER THIRTY EIGHT

A Long Time Coming

When we arrived it was sort of late, but not late enough for us not to eat. Terrance told me to sit down and relax. "I'm going to make you a quick and late light dinner." I sat on the sofa turned the television on and kicked back. I felt Terrance come up behind me and he started giving me a neck rub. It felt so good. It seemed all my tensions were being delightfully eased away.

"Man, that feels so good."

"I know, just relax." The food that Terrance was preparing was filling the air. The aroma tantalized my senses and I was getting hungry. "I have to go and check on our grub, would you like a glass of wine while you are waiting?"

"You know that would be nice, you are too good to me, best bud," I told him smiling.

"Okay, I'll be back in a minute." Terrance came back with my drink and handed it to me. "Hey, I didn't put anything in there that would make me lucky tonight, okay." He laughed.

"Very funny," I told him. He started preparing the table while I sipped on my drink. "Do you need any help?"

"No, I just need you to come and park it over here because dinner is served." Terrance went and turned the television off. "Do you want to hear some music?"

"That's a nice touch, yeah, that would nice." Terrance went and turned Teddy Pendergrass, *Come and Go With Me*. "Man, I haven't heard that one for awhile, but you know it's a nice classic." Terrance brought out a nice chicken Caesar salad and he had glazed chicken breast with rice pilaf on the side. He lit candles and turned the lights low. "Hey, man, what's up with this?"

"Come on, Shante, work with me. I just want you to know that out of everything you have been through, you will always be special to me, you're my best friend. Don't ever forget that." We picked up our wine glasses and lightly tapped them together.

"Everything was so tasty. I didn't know that you could cook like that."

"Hey, you never asked. It's a lot of things that I can do." We went back into the living room and sat on the couch. Terrance turned to me. "Remember the last time that you were over here and I made the wrong move on you?"

"Oh, Terrance, I never got mad about that."

"Yeah, well I'm sorry, but, Shante, I have been in love with you ever since I've known you."

Terrance reached over and started kissing me so intensely. I let all of my hurt feelings go and went with him, his tongue started t explore my mouth and I just lost my mind as the next track of Teddy singing, *"If you don't know me by now."* It all tied in together and I just went with it. I guess deep down I'd always had feelings for Terrance, but that night, they would not be pent up and held anymore. He unbuttoned my blouse and exposed my breast. He cupped them the utmost tenderness as he started kissing them simultaneously. He licked and sucked my nipples making me moan in complete pleasure. He looked at my expression of satisfaction and knew that I was definitely on the right road of my redemption. I stood up and walked slowly toward his bedroom while undoing my pants, stepping out of them as they dropped to the floor. Terrance started undoing his clothes and by the time we got to his bedroom, we were both butt naked and ready to engage in each other. I heard the CD player change. It was playing the O'Jays, *"You got your hooks in me."* Terrance embraced me with his enormous rod of pleasure in between us. He looked at me.

"Man, I've been waiting for this moment ever since I met you."

We passionately kissed then we fell on the bed with Terrance massaging my little oyster pleasure pearl. It wasn't long before I had produced enough juices for him to slip his fingers inside of me. He was driving me insane. He slipped in and out of me nearly drowning his fingers from my wetness. He pulled them out and asked me if I was ready.

"Yes, Terrance, please give it to me now, I want you now."

Terrance grabbed hold of his manhood and gently guided himself inside me. Our movements were perfectly in sync. He moaned with pure gratification. He found that spot that had yearning to be hit. When he hit it, I was driven into pure madness. I screamed in ecstasy.

"Yeah, baby, let it go, don't hold back, your pussy feels good squeezing my dick." I felt the last eruption from him when he powerfully thrust forward to empty his engorged muscle within me. We both arrived at that place together. Terrance yelled out, "I'm going to cum in you puss.." and we erupted together, groaning and moaning. Terrance was left breathing hard while his sweat rolled off of his glistening skin unto me. He stroked my skin as we turned to each other and exchanged smiles of happiness.

CHAPTER THIRTY NINE

Time To Synchronize Watches

Morning came and I woke up to the smell of bacon and eggs welcoming me into a new, wonderful day. I sat up and savored the smell of the breakfast that Terrance was cooking. Sadness fell over me as I thought about where my life was that morning compared to months ago. It had dissolved and crumbled in a manner of seconds it seemed. I thought about how ruthless people were in the world. I thought about that time when I heard that conversation I heard that day in the nail salon. Marriage was not sacred anymore. If someone wanted what you got, then they would just take it. Deception was a mutha. I knew I had been thrown into the cycle of deceit because of what I have done with Terrance, but it was like a domino effect. I was knocked down with all the rest. But, I know that it really happened from me being naïve most of my life. There was no point of me crying over spilled milk. From now on, I was going to open my eyes and look only forward more toward my future.

Terrence came bringing a tray with a wonderful breakfast on it. "Oh, girl, I was trying to beat you and surprise you with this breakfast."

"Oh, that is so sweet."

"No, we have to do this the right way. Swing around and get back in bed."

I smiled. "Okay, have it your way." He brought the tray to the bed. He had eggs, bacon, toast, and cherries in a crystal glass and fresh cut flowers in the middle for presentation. "This is perfect." We both dug in and ate while we talked.

"Did Steve give you a call yet?"

"No he said two days, which would mean calling tomorrow. You know, Terrance, I'm getting so nervous. I know that Melvin has been trying to call me. He has never gone so long without talking to me. He is probably going crazy not knowing where I am."

"Don't worry about it. He really doesn't know about whom I am and where I live. I want you to feel safe."

"But, Terrance, you don't know him like I do. Yesterday I felt safe, but today I feel a little scared."

"Look, if it will make you feel any better I'll give Steve a call later and ask him for an update. Will that make you feel any better?"

"Yes, that would make me feel a whole lot better."

"Come on now, let's eat before this food I cooked for us gets cold."

Terrance cell phone rang and it was Steve. "Hey, speak of the devil, it is Steve. He beat us to the punch." My heart sank as Terrance answered the phone. "Hey, Steve, what's up?"

"Hey, I just wanted to call you all and give you an update on the situation. I checked out the couple that Melvin and you had befriended while on the Islands, well I had my assistant to check out the guest list and they used a different names on the flight they took out their compared to the names they used when they checked in. From the hotel registration, they went by Roy and Alisha Clark. But, their real names were Thomas Bryant and Brenda Smalls. And, check this out, they both work for Fun Productions right along with Melvin. So, they knew what they were doing. This little trip was all a set up. They wanted you to believe that you all had just met. Then, they set you up on that booze cruise to drug you and set you up with that movie and photos."

"But, why would he do that? How can you say you love me and watch other people have their way with me while you were watching?"

"That part gets me, too. He probably thought that you would never want that stuff to be shown to anybody. And, that you would clam up and continue your life without much fuss. Now, as far as the bank account, do you know exactly when he is due back?"

"It should be Friday."

"Have you decided on where you want to go, because you may have to make a far journey if we pull this off."

"I still want to go to the Virgin Islands."

"Are you sure about this?"

"Yes."

"Hold on, Jeanine, call the travel agent and book a fight for the Virgin Islands, probably around twelve or one in the afternoon." My heart started beating fast. I couldn't believe it. I was really going to leave. "Okay, Shante, are you absolutely sure you have not contacted or talked to anyone since you left your house yesterday."

"I'm positive."

"Alright, this is the plan. Tomorrow, I want you to go to the bank and close that account at Mellon Bank that Melvin has the money in."

"I'm really nervous now. Do you know he has about four hundred and eight thousand in there? He would probably kill me if I took all of his money."

"Okay, would it make you feel any better if you left him a couple of thousands in there?"

"Well I..."

"Come on, Shante, I know you are not getting soft on me, after all this nigger has put you through. He owes you that money, just for being such a liar to you all of your life."

"Okay, what is it that I should do?"

"Tomorrow, go to the bank and go directly to one desk with a name plate on it, Yolanda Brown. She's a lovely, chocolate skinned sister with neat looking dreads. She will hold a conversation with you and pretend to be on the computer doing a transaction for you. She is already going to have your check drawn up for you. Does that make you feel better? This is the beauty of this plan. We can trust her, she owes me. She will be expecting you. When you are finished there, go back to Terrance's house and wait until we call you and tell you what time for you to catch your flight. Someone there will come up to you and give you your ticket. Oh yeah, they are going to have a new cell phone for you also for you to communicate on. And, don't forget you can't call anyone and give them any clues to where you are."

Steve had thought of everything. My stomach was still a little nervous. I gave Terrance the phone back and he took it out of the room and continued to talk to him about small details. After Terrance finished talking with Steve, he filled me in the plan and made sure that I understood everything.

"Terrance, I'm scared. I mean, I want to start over, but I don't know if I can do it by myself. And, what am I going to do without you?"

"Come on now, let's think positive. You know I will miss you, but every chance I get I will be over there with you, I promise. Come on now, be brave. I'm only going to be a phone call away." Terrance put his arm around me and made me feel safe again. We looked in each other's eyes and knew we wanted to feel what we had felt just last night. In a matter of seconds, Terrance had taken me back there and all the sad memories and fear had been erased.

It was finally here, the time of my redemption, deliverance, my freedom. Terrance lay right behind me still asleep with his arm still wrapped around me. The alarm went off. "Ummm, is it time to get up already? Good morning, babe. Man, you really drained me good last night." Terrance kissed me on my shoulder.

"Good morning."

"I guess we better do what we have to do." I turned around to him. "You know, Terrance, I wish I had the power to freeze time. We would be here forever. But, as soon as I walk out the door, my reality with rear its ugly head. Terrance, I'm still scared as shit. If Melvin ever gets to me, I know he is going to kill me. It won't be no and, ifs, or buts about it, I'm as good as dead."

"Come on now, babe, I'll still be with you. You can always call. I will definitely call you." Terrance kissed me. "It's the only way now." The phone rang and Terrance answered it. "Hello how is everything going this morning?" It was Steve so he put the phone on speaker.

"It's all good. Everything is taken care of. Your flight leaves at eleven this morning. It probably will take you about an hour to get there, it's going to be cutting it close, but that's the best I could do. There will be a girl waiting at the entrance with your tickets and cell phone. She knows you, Terrance, so don't worry. I'll call you to check on you alright?"

"Okay let's do this."

Terrance and I were almost out the door when I thought about my camera. "Wait." I pulled it out of my purse. "Hey, smile for me." I snapped a photo of Terrance.

"Come on, girl, we only don't have any minutes to spare."

We rushed to the car and went downtown to Mellon Bank. Terrance told me that he would wait outside for me. When I got inside and walked by a handsome security guard. "Good morning."

"Good morning," I greeted him back.

I saw a friendly face sitting behind the desk with the name of Yolanda Brown. She looked up with a smile. "Good morning, may I help you?" She sounded so official that I got nervous, hell I didn't know if she knew what was going on.

"Hi, I wanted to ask about closing an account."

"Sure, can you give me your account number and fill this form out please?" When she gave me the form it had just go with the flow and pretend. I gave her Melvin's ID card. "Okay just give me a minute." She walked over to the copier and made a photo of the ID. When she sat back down she pushed the paper back to me. She didn't even make a copy. She was keying information into the computer, then looked at me and slipped me an envelope on the front saying your check is inside.

In the car I got quiet because I wanted to talk to my sister so bad. Terrance looked over at me and knew what I was thinking from the solemn look that came over my face. "Look, Sharise, I promise you one day that you will be able to talk to your sister, but right now it is not the right time because of your safety."

"I know, but you know it's hard."

"Trust me on this, it's going to be okay."

When we pulled up to the airport, Terrance parked the car as I started looking through my purse to make sure that I had everything. Suddenly, on an inside pocket I came across a decent photo that Melvin and I had taken on the Island. That look was again upon my face. "What is it, Shante? You know today I just can't keep you happy. Every minute you just keep changing, what is it?" I pulled the photo out and showed it to Terrance. "Oh, this is how he looks with clothes on." He was trying to cheer me up. He did bring a smile on my face. "Come on now we promise that we were going to move forward from now on, agreed?"

"Okay. Here you can dispose of it for me." I handed him the photo. "Okay let's rock." We got out of the car, Terrence went in the trunk and got my suitcase and we started walking up to the entrance, and just as Steve said, someone from the office was standing outside the door with a big smile because it was a friend of Terrence.

"Hey, what's up, girl?"

"Oh nothing, here are the materials you needed. He said that he will call you in about four hours and for you to enjoy yourself."

I took the big envelope and thanked her. As we walked in, Terrence was telling her that he would talk to her later. Inside the envelope were my ticket and a new cell phone. He was true to his word. I looked at the clock and it was thirty minutes before I had to board.

Terrence put the suitcase on the belt and we walked over to a restaurant to grab something real quick. He saw a small table in the corner and asked the waitress could we sit there. "Of course, sir, come this way." She seated us at a table that Terrence had requested. He looked at me and saw that I was still just a little nervous. He held his hand up to signal the waitress.

"Yes, could you bring a gin and tonic and a frozen margarita?"

"Would you salt around the rim and a lime?" He looked at me and I told her yes.

"Thanks, Terrance. " He looked at his watch and told me that we had thirty minutes. When our drinks came, I sipped it with my straw and ran my finger around the rim to taste a little salt with my drink. I took the straw out and ran my tongue across it to taste the frosty treat. "Ummm, that's so good."

"You know that's not even right to tease me with that drink."

"What? I'm just enjoying the drink you bought me because it's so good." Terrance smiled as he sipped through his straw. I was feeling a little tipsy already because of the rush we had to do. Terrance reached across the table and held my hand.

"I'm going to miss you so much, but you best to believe we will talk every day. I promise."

"I am going to hold you to that."

I had five minutes left to get in line for the plane. Terrance paid for our drinks and we proceeded to the line for me to board. We held hands as we stepped into the line. The passengers from a plane that had landed ten minutes ago were coming in to form a line inside to get their luggage. The exit door for us to start to leave out was leading passengers out to their plane. Terrence's attention was directed to a tall gentleman that he had recognized just from a few moments ago, from the photo that I had just showed him. It was Melvin walking toward us. He had just got off the plane that came in. Terrance quickly turned me around and slobbered me down so Melvin could not see my face. His quick thinking paid off. Melvin didn't recognize me and he had never seen Terrence's before. When he was out of view, I had to ask what in the world had come over him, he ran down what had just happened, gave me one last kiss, and I was off boarding the plane.

CHAPTER FOURTY

Final Touches

On the plane, that margarita had helped calmed my nerves down. I closed my eyes and dreamed of the soothing waters that I hoped to see. My nerves jumped again as I thought about Melvin. I grabbed my purse and looked in it again to make sure my check was there. It was safe and sound. I closed my eyes once again and the images of Melvin in that film disturbed my dreams. I prayed to let these images leave me for once and for all. The plane finally was touching down. I looked out my window at the beautiful scenery. I was finally there, a place I wanted to call home.

It was Monday afternoon and I got a call from Steve. "Hello."

"Hello, Shante, it's over, you are a free woman. He agreed to everything, but I still want you to lay low for awhile before calling anyone. I know you are concerned about Sharise, but I will fill her in and still won't discuss your whereabouts just yet. How are you doing down there?"

"I'm doing great. The water and beaches is to die for. I've found a house right on the beach that I am renting. In these few days, I have finished something that I have never been able to finish until now."

"Yeah what's that?"

"A poem."

"Really? Recite it to me."

"Okay it's called, *A Satisfied Black Woman.*"

A satisfied Black woman
Will I ever know?
A lifetime of thinking and wondering
Which way I really should go
The road I left behind

Both joys and sorrows it held
The road that stands before me
Holds mysteries
Unknown tales
Sometimes good, sometimes bad
Is what I have been told
A satisfied black woman
Will I ever know?
If I hold on to my dreams
And promise to never let go
Will my efforts be rewarded?
Or will anybody ever know?
Don't criticize me when,
I stop along the way
There are lessons I must learn
Sometimes my heart will pay
As life goes on it teaches me
To look beyond one's soul
To guard against the hurt and blows
That sometimes may unfold
A satisfied black woman
I hope one day I'll know

Just as I finished the last line of my poem, a shadow came up behind me. The warm rays of the sun had been blocked from a person's shadow that was standing right behind me. I figured it was an islander trying to sell me something, or even try and have a fling with me for a little money. They were always trying something over here. I turned slightly and saw that popular plaid Polo tennis shoe that I'd only knew one person to wear. I turned all the way around and I dropped the phone, thinking that I was seeing a mirage. It was Terrance smiling.

"Hell, I couldn't live one more second without you. I guess you are stuck with me on this Island." We embraced each other so tightly. Terrence looked at me and asked me how I felt.

I told him that I felt like, "A satisfied Black woman."

The End

LaVergne, TN USA
04 December 2009
166025LV00006B/93/P